Judging Me

Hon.
**Mary
Elizabeth
Bullock**
(Retired)

Copyright © 2013 by Mary Elizabeth Bullock

All rights reserved.

ISBN: 1489593373
ISBN-13: 9781489593375
Library of Congress Control Number: 2013915574
CreateSpace Independent Publishing Platform
North Charleston, South Carolina

CHAPTER TITLES

Dedication		vii
Foreword		xi
Prologue		xv
Chapter 1	Introduction	1
Chapter 2	My Story in the Making	5
Chapter 3	A Primer on Childhood Sexual Abuse	9
Chapter 4	My Family	15
Chapter 5	Why Do We Feel So Uncomfortable With This Story?	21
Chapter 6	An Unprecedented War Zone	23
Chapter 7	Motels Along The Way	27
Chapter 8	Boundaries	29
Chapter 9	A Temporary Respite	33
Chapter 10	Adolescence	35
Chapter 11	Does the Story Ever End?	41
Chapter 12	A Visionary	49

Chapter 13	The Devil Made Me Do It	57
Chapter 14	Stuck in the Moment	63
Chapter 15	Metamorphosis	69
Chapter 16	Thriving Through Crises Takes Monumental Courage	77
Chapter 17	Reflect, Reveal, and Revel	83
Chapter 18	The Bed	99
Chapter 19	Revenge for the Sins of My Father	103
Chapter 20	Therapy	123
Chapter 21	Why Law School?	127
Chapter 22	Law School	131
Chapter 23	A Woman's Viewpoint of the Law	137
Chapter 24	My Philosophy of Law	141
Chapter 25	"The Subconscious Is The Key To One's Life's Pursuits."	145
Chapter 26	Birth of the EEOC	151
Chapter 27	Full Circle	157

Author's Note: Some of the content of the book is graphic in nature due to the harsh realities of the subject matter. A portion of the proceeds from the sale of this book will go to organizations that help sexually abused children and survivors. Thank you for being a part of this endeavor.

Respectfully submitted,

Mary E. Bullock

Honorable Mary Elizabeth Bullock (Retired)

DEDICATION

Judging Me is dedicated to my children: my daughter, Kristie, who helped shape the book, kept me together when precious little else did, and rallied for the publication of a story she truly believed would help others as I struggled to write my truth and to my son, Mike, who supported me through thick and thin.

This book is further dedicated to the forty-two million survivors who, according to the Center for Disease Control, suffer from sexual abuse: a malignant cancer that still manages to lurk in our society relatively unnoticed and that victimizes one in every six young boys and one in every four little girls[1].

---

1 The estimated numbers of sexual abuse cited by various federal and state agencies vary from thirty-six million to forty-two million. Since many instances go unreported the numbers are assumed to be higher.

INVICTUS

Out of the night that covers me,
Black as the Pit from pole to pole,
I thank whatever gods may be
For my unconquerable soul.

In the fell clutch of circumstance
I have not winced or cried aloud,
Under the bludgeoning of chance
My head is bloody but unbowed

Beyond this place of wrath and tears
Looms but the Horror of the shade,
And yet the menace of the years
Finds, and shall find, me unafraid.

It matters not how strait the gate,
How charged with punishments the scroll,
I am the master of my fate:
I am the captain of my soul.

—Williams Ernest Henley

FOREWORD

In no way does this book condone the judgment of other people. I am uniquely qualified to judge myself and only myself. The dissonance in my life created a need to seek out the truth. The transformation of a violently, sexually abused child into the formidable woman I became beats the odds in life. This metamorphosis necessitated a search of my soul. No one can walk in the shoes of another person without inherent biases and prejudices. Until the world is in perfect order and each of us is in harmony with all humankind, not one of us can remotely begin to grasp what transpires in the hearts of other people. We must accept that there are mysteries of the heart that no one can truly predict or understand.

There is a common theme that runs throughout this book. When bad things happen to good people and never let up, the question must be asked—and answered: "What did they do in this life or any other life to deserve this? Is this their fault, or did fate just chose them at random?" Humankind has searched an eternity for answers.

A life of injustices, abuse, betrayal, and deceit made me who I am. The refining fire—or the testing of one's mettle—has only honed my unique skill set and sharpened my purpose. It is no longer enough to survive through the tragedies and absurdities of life. As people, we must strive for a higher goal: to thrive—regardless of what life hands us. There is a quantum leap between surviving and thriving. How does a person who has valiantly suffered through life's ironies thrive? It is through a sense of filial duty to a worthy cause that binds us to a higher plateau and the honor that is given to that commitment.

A woman who, as a child, experienced incest and extreme sexual abuse is never completely healed. She becomes quick to sense betrayal and fast to spot hypocrisy. She is especially sensitive to relations of hierarchy and power. She remains highly vulnerable to suffering. She sometimes chooses the path of suffering as a means of confirming her ability to survive. If she is smart and strong, she discovers that grievances permeate society and do not exist entirely as her cross to bear. She then declares to stand on the side of social justice, to dedicate herself as a change agent, and to pursue the causes of the dispirited and disadvantaged. For her, every day is a personal struggle, for the crimes of the past never go away.

I am that woman.

My narrative begins with the abuses of my father. It proceeds through my often-failing efforts to construct supportive personal relationships, through my relationships in the bedroom—seeking revenge for the sins of my father—through law school, and through the practice of law. It continues through my appointment as a federal civil rights judge working for the United States Equal Employment Opportunity Commission (EEOC), whose mission is to "eradicate all vestiges of discrimination." This is a book for our times: where sexual abuse runs rampant in our society and where blind eyes turn horrific events into the destruction of a child's soul.

The title of this book is *Judging Me*, or *Judging M(ary) E(lizabeth)*. This is what I tried to do, and it was a painful task. There is much in these pages that is not pretty. There are behaviors that

Foreword

I certainly regret. There are harsh condemnations: toward my father, who perpetrated repeated rapes upon me and sold me to others for their sexual pleasure, and toward my family that ignored everything; toward the men who passed through my bed without affecting my soul; and toward myself and my weaknesses and inadequacies. This book is my effort to wrestle through the atrocities perpetrated upon me. In essence, it is dedicated to a continued struggle and to turning struggles into personal achievements.

A person who struggles makes mistakes and can be blindsided—no matter how well-intentioned. The lesson of struggle for me was to turn the dramatic tensions into a social commitment for justice. This book is raw, gritty, and assiduous—much like me. I do not make excuses for what and why things happened, nor do I find the child I once was blameworthy. In the end, however, I am ultimately responsible for my actions and myself. Make no mistake: I am my worst critic.

As a federal civil rights judge, I did not judge people but rather situations where one party felt wronged by the other—snapshots in time. As a judge, I was responsible for being open-minded, for weighing evidence carefully, for understanding that not all arguments are equally valid, for setting aside personal predispositions, and for coming to a reasoned decision based on the merits of the case. I have tried to maintain this very same perspective when assessing the course of my life's journey. In revealing myself through these pages, I have placed my life on brutal display. The black suits and judicial robes have literally and figuratively been cast aside. My underbelly exposed. I promise when I read your story, I will not judge you—you have probably judged yourself a hundred times and punished yourself ten times over. I know I did. I ask that you be as compassionate with me as I am with you, my reader. If you choose to judge me, my request is for sympathetic understanding—for myself and, by extension, for all those others who fell victim to betrayal, abuse, and hypocrisy.

My name is Mary Elizabeth, and this is my journey.

PROLOGUE

The word *prologue* comes from the Greek word meaning "before the discourse:" a course of action foreshadowing greater events. The past is the architect of the present. The question is whether the past will dictate the future. Woven in the tapestry of my life, there were life-altering experiences that profoundly changed my course. My response to this particular experience spoke volumes.

───

"I will fucking kill you, and you know I will. Your body and car will disappear one day. But before I kill you, I will torture you: just the way your old man did—just the way you like it," he whispered. I froze. I knew with dead certainty that he was serious. Was I partly to blame for this man's madness? Had I finally found my Mr. Goodbar? Somehow, I knew my life was at the edge.

After he left, I telephoned the police department, and the operator connected me to the District Attorney's Special Threats Unit. A young male assistant with the district attorney kept asking me for my name. I was still so shocked, I could not respond. When I could not say my name, he asked, "Who threatened you?" My brain temporarily unfroze. It was then I realized that I could not give him my name. I was a public figure. A different kind of paralyzing panic swept through me as the young man asked me for the man's social security number, address, telephone number—even his date of birth.

I relayed that I did not know when he was born. Perplexed and agitated, the young man stated, "Miss, I find it hard to believe that you have been dating this man for three years, and you don't even know his birthday." Angry now—a sharp edge to my voice—I replied, "In all due respect, sir, I have been fucking this man for three years, and his birthday was irrelevant." Silence. Finally, I whispered, "This telephone call was a mistake; I need to think this through and call you back."

I knew this young man was trying to help me. In a voice barely above a whisper he said, "What is there to think about? He will kill you when he can. You are scared; I hear it in your voice. It's just a matter of time before he makes good on his threats."

For one sane second, I almost came clean, and then I realized why telling him was impossible. I could not wrap my mind around ruining this man's life forever; yet, was my own self-loathing so great that I was willing to let him take mine?

What was wrong with this picture? Plenty, I knew. How in God's name did my life ever get to this point?

INTRODUCTION

They say we are all born the same. To some extent, I believe that is true. It has also been said that, at some point, some of us just become more interesting. This is simply not true. At some time or another, horrible things happen to people—it is part of the human condition. Someone said that life is a hell of a thing to happen to a person. I wonder if the author of that statement really understood just how profound that statement was. How a person struggles through adversity proves what kind of mettle he or she is made of. Each of us has a story to tell—if only others would listen. The collage of my life is dark and depraved; it is complex and complicated with layers of savagery and brutality that shock the conscience.

In general, good people want to believe that their neighborhoods and fellow human beings are not capable of gross atrocities to their own flesh and blood: the innocents—their own babies and children. They are wrong. I had neighbors; yet, I dare say they never had a glimpse of the horrors that transpired in my house. We all want to believe in innocence and love, and that there are rules that our society follows because we are not animals, but we are civilized: with advanced technologies and insights into human nature. As a country, we are both loving and God-fearing. In that blanket of security, we sleep peacefully, while the serial rapists of our nation are shaped in those little houses of horror. We work hard at our respective jobs and sleep soundly into the night. Believing that people are, for the most part, good, we are able to wake to a new day and start the cycle of living once again. Make no mistake: to think that our world is not dangerous to the unsuspecting is a form of delusion and self-deception. It is what we want to believe as a society, or we will go insane. Most people live their lives in total bliss and ignorance. If we were truly aware of what went on in other little houses of horror—next door and in our own neighborhoods—we would fear for our very safety and that of our children: paralyzed by the fear of tomorrow's monsters.

I grew up in a house of horrors. Were it not for the love of a Power greater than myself and the grace He bestowed upon me, I would not have turned out to be the exception to statistics and case studies—extraordinary in my own way. When asked to write this book, I did it to search for an answer as to why I mercifully became who and what I am—unlike others with similar circumstances who were less fortunate when all of life's variables were the same.

My father sadistically raped me, sodomized me, and forced me to have sex with total strangers and physical objects for ten-plus years. Fostered by a violent man, I have that violence in me. The difference is that I do not let it loose whenever I feel like it—on whoever is handy. There is something in me that stops that: which makes me decent. I know that, realistically, I am who I am because of what I was and, more importantly, what I have made of myself. Whatever he did to me, he could not make me what he was. Scars tell us where we have been; they do not dictate where we are going. I made myself. So shall you, my reader. Never discount the human soul's ability to confront and disarm the polarities in life that often bring human endeavors to an impasse.

I cannot really tell you why—much like a parable—a seed that grows from the cracks of a sidewalk flourishes: even through angry

Introduction

rains and thoughtless people who carelessly crush the new growth. Imagine a gardener, the caretaker of a large estate, preparing a new soil bed in an elaborate and well-tended garden. In spring, the caretaker prepares the garden by planting new seeds. Through no fault of the gardener, a gust of wind comes along and scatters one of the seeds into the crack of a sidewalk. The seed, unable to find purchase, cannot form deep roots. While the gardener routinely nourishes and nurtures the seedlings' soil, no nurturing or nourishment is available to the lone seed—except by accidents of nature. Still, the seed grows into a beautiful and miraculous flower. Who knows why some of the seeds that are well-tended do not grow to their full potential. Sometimes, weeds grow up and strangle the seedlings, or gophers attack the roots from below the soil. Yet, the remaining seeds grow—together—filling the flowerbed with an abundance of color. The flowers are not as beautiful as the sole flower growing through the crack. There is something heroic about this flower's growth: a seedling making it against all odds. Perhaps, that is the where and why the flower takes on a special glow of its own. Who is to say?

Life's greatest question comes from the how and why each of us became who and what we are today. As each of us grows into adulthood—regardless of the environment or surroundings—beauty and goodness may appear from the least-expected places. Perhaps my story will help explain that a strong belief in a Higher Power can make all the difference in a person's life. To those who suffer as I write and to those who suffered in the past, may this story bring you closer to a journey of redemption, new beginnings, second chances, and personal empowerment.

MY STORY IN THE MAKING

Our minds sanitize the truth so we can cope. I did not want the sanitized version of the events. I would rather have eaten my spleen. The truth for me is far more tolerable than a fantasy I have no inner structure to support. I understand why the abused place a different face on the series of events that is more tolerable to themselves, friends, family, and society. It was not a mask I could adorn without suffocation.

Writing this book was in no way cathartic. I did not expect it to be. What I did not expect (and what ultimately blindsided me) were the powerful emotions that surfaced. I felt sheer unmitigated rage combined with convulsions of anger that almost paralyzed me from being able to screw my butt into the chair and finish this book. After all, powerful emotions get in the way of living our lives. As a result, we try to keep those types of emotions at bay. When I first understood what was happening to me, I believed it was as simple as grist for the mill.

It was not that way at all. I was left with a lap full of ugly and grotesque emotions that I had no way of dealing with or of finding any way to keep them in check. Raging around my apartment (like some mad lunatic in the middle of a temper tantrum) and destroying precious keepsakes was no solution. It would indeed have made me feel even worse. Self-help remedies aimed at those responsible for my rage—such as putting a knot on their heads—were illegal. Thus, working these feelings out was a slow, grinding process that extracted enormous amounts of energy. As a result, I turned to prayer. I sweated bullets to get through this and found that only through forgiveness of myself could I break the dam that nearly broke me. This was the hardest thing I have ever done—especially when those responsible for these powerful emotions repeatedly ripped the scabs from wounds that never truly healed. Coming to terms with real monsters is an act of bravery and humility. The only thing that really mattered was that I had a story to tell that I was certain would help others, and when push came to shove, I shoved through the insanity and glued my butt into the chair.

The fact that I survived as a child through unspeakable acts of sexual violence speaks more to my strength of character than to any turn of life's events. It serves no one to speak only of the horrors. The publication of my story is to empower and encourage the disillusioned, dispossessed, disenfranchised, and those without a feather of hope. The human condition is inescapable and inextricable. It serves everyone to speak of the power of courage, faith, perseverance, dreams, a sense of humor, and an endless ability to seek the good out from under the bad; to unconditionally embrace love; and to aggressively pursue a different kind of life. Indeed, for me, it has been a lifelong commitment.

There is no question that I live my life to the beat of a different drummer. Change agents are ordinary human beings whose lives—inadvertently and without warning—force them to make decisions, which, in hindsight, become extraordinary acts of courage. My story reads like that. At the age of six, my father tied me to a palm tree in a snake-infested swamp because I refused to choke down his cum. I prayed that God would end a very vicious pattern of destruction that—as a child—I could find no way to understand or control.

My Story In The Making

God took my life and formed it in such a way that the publication of this book became a soul-driven imperative. His purpose—and now mine—was so simple: if I could take the debris of my life and fashion it in such a way that I helped just one other person, then what happened to me was not in vain.

My greatest strength in life was exemplified by my ability to balance the considerable discord between the violently sexually abused child I was and the formidable woman I became: a federal civil rights judge. The cognitive dissonance between my two worlds would have smothered the best of souls. Initially, my survival depended on my ability to keep my worlds apart. The obvious consequences of not balancing the two worlds as they eventually emerged into one would have ended in a collision of cataclysmic proportion—a certainty of life.

As a child, I was poor and powerless—vulnerable in place and time. Told all of my life that I was nothing, I discovered in myself a deeper sense of me—something so pure with a potential for love. The thought of such a radically new sense of self brought me to ponder the immense and wondrous possibilities of this deeper reality. There is something in me that no man can touch: that belongs to me and to God—inaccessible to the brutalities of my life. I became cognizant of myself as valuable, unique, and undiminishable at the core. This truth was a liberating force. Making a commitment to the deeper reality of myself, I proceeded in life without knowing much about what it would entail or where it would lead. My response to this deeper self was to say, "Yes." It changed my life forever.

Not one person could fathom the years I lived. No one knew how those events unfolded in my life, reverberated back to me in every endeavor, and rippled outward. Guilt demanded I be punished; grief moved, honed, and sharpened me. Disassociation disconnected me from the real world, spouses, children, and friends. The search for healthy boundaries between myself and others and the nature of their relationship to me was overwhelming. I easily lost my center. I spent nearly a lifetime in search of what and who I was. The perplexities of life and its unpredictability left me in a storm of chaos in search of calmer waters.

A PRIMER ON CHILDHOOD SEXUAL ABUSE

Childhood sexual abuse is not a disease or disorder but rather an experience. A sexual act is imposed upon a child who lacks maturation and emotional and cognitive development. Authority and power, silence and secrecy enable the perpetrator to coerce the child into sexual compliance.

This book focuses on familial childhood sexual abuse. Familial relationships—such as incest (for example, father and daughter or son), uncles, other close family relatives, or close family friends—are one type of abuse. Incest is the most common type of childhood sexual abuse. Most sex between children and adults involves a grooming process in which the adult, known by the child, skillfully manipulates a child into participating in a sexual act.

Sexual abuse has been defined in a variety of ways by various clinicians. Most experts would agree that there are many forms of familial childhood sexual abuse. However, the experts generally define sexual abuse as the exploitation, seduction, suggestion, or coercion of a child or younger adult by another person who dominates and demands sexual activity.[2] Irrespective of how abuse is defined, studies have consistently demonstrated that childhood sexual abuse is associated with a wide range of behavioral, psychological, and physical problems. These problems persist into adulthood and have a significant and pervasive impact.

Childhood sexual abuse infringes on the basic right of a child to be free from unwanted and inappropriate sexual encounters ranging from actual penetration to Internet trolling and manipulation of the child into taking pornographic photos. Children should be able to have sexual experiences at the right developmental time and within their control and choices.

The nature and dynamics of sexual abuse and sexually abusive relationships are traumatic and long lasting. When sexual abuse occurs in childhood, it hinders normal social growth and is the cause of many different psychosocial problems.

Survivors often experience a toxic mix of guilt, shame, and self-blame. It has been clinically demonstrated that survivors frequently take personal responsibility for the abuse. When the sexual abuse was committed by an esteemed, loved adult, it may be hard for a child to view the perpetrator in a negative light. He or she has difficulty in externalizing the abuse; thus, the child thinks negatively about himself or herself. In other words, the abused feels as if it was his or her fault and takes on personal responsibility accordingly.

---

2 Author's note: This book was not written as an intellectual endeavor, *per se*. The author concludes that the definitions that experts hale as necessary and sufficient for sexual abuse are weak and pathetic. Where, I must ask, are the outrage and the bloodcurdling screams that come from such an atrocious act perpetrated on a child? Where is the horror? Significantly absent. The author understands that any definition is flatlined and can only be aided by proper adjectives and further explanation; even then, the definition remains two-dimensional. Since this book is not an academic treatise, the remaining sections of this chapter delve into symptomotology.

A Primer On Childhood Sexual Abuse

In determining the nature and severity of the abuse, it is important to know several factors: who the perpetrator was or the different relationships it could be associated with; the number of incidents; the frequency with which the abuse occurred; the variation in circumstances; and the age of the victim when the abuse began. The more extensive the sexual abuse, the greater number of incidents; and the younger the child, the more seriously impaired the adult survivor.

There are other differences that will affect the victim and the degree of damage he or she suffers afterward. These factors are as follows: the perspective of the survivor; the individual's internal resources; and the individual's level of support. A victim that has a large support system and a stockpile of internal resources will fare much better than the victim who has no support and lacks the internal resources to sort through the intense feelings and consequences that come from sexual abuse.

Childhood sexual abuse is correlated with the following: higher levels of depression, guilt, self-blame, severe eating disorders (anorexia and bulimia), somatic concerns, anxiety, dissociative patterns, repression, denial, sexual problems, and relationship issues. It is important to remember that there is no singular symptomatic definition for sexual abuse. However, the severity and significant indicators it has on the everyday life of the survivors is well documented. There are life-altering consequences for the sexually abused. Understanding these consequences is tantamount to healing and new beginnings.

Depression is a lifelong symptom of child abuse. When the survivor cannot externalize the abuser, he or she will internalize the pain and become profoundly depressed. Depression, by definition, is anger turned inward. This leads to thoughts of being unlovable, undesirable, and unworthy. After years of negative self-talk, survivors will avoid others and often refuse to leave the safety of their homes. Besides feeling down most of the time, they experience suicidal ideation, eating disorders, and disturbed sleep patterns. Survivors tend to display more suicidal ideation than those who have not been abused.

Body issues and eating disorders have also been cited as long-term effects of childhood abuse. Body-image problems surface as a feeling of being dirty or ugly, dissatisfaction with one's body appearance, severe eating disorders (as described above), and obesity. Somatic concerns are problematic for the abused.

Some survivors suffer from extreme stress and chronic anxiety in their everyday life. Childhood sexual abuse can be frightening and stressful long after the abusive event ends. It is not unusual for symptoms to surface after an extended period of time following the abuse or after cumulative traumas. Survivors then experience chronic anxiety, tension, panic attacks, and phobias. A study compared the post-traumatic stress symptoms in Vietnam veterans to adult survivors of childhood abuse. The study revealed that childhood sexual abuse is traumatizing and can result in symptoms comparable to symptoms from war-related trauma. This study was done by J. McNew and N. Abell in 1995 in an article titled "Posttraumatic Stress Symptomology: Similarities and Differences between Vietnam Veterans and Adult Survivors of Childhood Sexual Abuse," published in *Social Work* (Volume 40, Issue 1, pages 115–126).

Dissociation, a coping mechanism, is used when the abused feel unsafe or threatened. Dissociation includes feelings of confusion, disorientation, nightmares, flashbacks, and difficulty experiencing feelings. Denial and repression of sexual abuse is seen to be another long-term effect of childhood sexual abuse. Symptoms include: experiencing amnesia, minimizing the impact and effects of sexual abuse, and feeling that what happened in the past should be forgotten.

Survivors of sexual abuse may experience difficulty in establishing long-term interpersonal relationships. The abuse itself hinders and blocks the development and growth of relationships. The most common forms of difficulty show up in the following areas: trust or trusting, fear of intimacy, difficulty establishing interpersonal boundaries, or getting involved in abusive relationships. Survivors also struggle with hierarchy and authority. It is difficult to say no when there is an abuse of power. Survivors are often prime candidates for adult victimization: such as sexual harassment or exploitation in the workforce. It is difficult for survivors to firmly assert themselves through the use of the word *no*. The word *no* is a complete sentence and should need no further elucidation. *No* means no. However, in the real world, the perpetrator shows no intention of respecting the potential victim's desires. Studies have also shown that an abused person has a propensity to select abusive employers. As the severity of the sexual abuse increases, the ability to adjust to intimate relationships decreases.

Many survivors of sexual abuse suffer sexual difficulties. The sexual symptoms present as: avoiding, fearing, or lacking interest in sex; approaching sex as an obligation; experiencing negative feelings such as anger, disgust, or guilt with touch; having difficulty becoming aroused or feeling sensation; feeling emotionally distant or not present during sex; experiencing intrusive or disturbing sexual thoughts; engaging in compulsive or inappropriate sexual behaviors; experiencing difficulty establishing or maintaining an intimate relationship; experiencing vaginal pain or orgasmic difficulties; having flashbacks; and sexually displaying sadistic or masochistic tendencies.

It is imperative that more studies be conducted to expand our knowledge of sexual abuse. Without a doubt, more research is needed to address the best practices and treatments for the abused survivor. Education is paramount to preventing more victims.

The secrecy and silence of sexual abuse must be eliminated, and society must take measures to prevent abuse—regardless of potential fallout. While sexual abuse remains a taboo topic, this cancer will continue to spread in epidemic proportions. Without a thorough analysis of abuse, survivors and victims will never be able to stop the victimization process or to properly heal. Clinical studies and observations are important in understanding what happens to others and people like myself.

The above discussion was a very brief summary of cumulative research that I found consistent with what others and I have experienced. The range and severity of symptoms are daunting. It is important to find a good therapist that converses with—rather than simply medicates—the abused. Talk therapy combined with medication is one of the most successful models for therapy. Drugs alone are never sufficient, as they merely mask the internal turmoil.

In the closing of this chapter, I believe it is vitally important to wake up all Americans to the tragedy of childhood sexual abuse. In my effort to embrace, not just myself, but all those who have suffered or are suffering from sexual abuse, my research revealed that the history of societal change towards the abused is gritty. Much like grains of sand that build up over time, the topic of sexual abuse will eventually tip the scales or alter the terrain. Real education about the topic is an uphill battle. The preciousness of life is never clearer to me than it is now. The beauty of life and the fragility of a child is real. Yet, I witnessed in myself and others an unbendable spirit where strength and optimism burns deep from within.

MY FAMILY

Webster's Dictionary defines the family as two adults with children. Other dictionaries add superlatives to the meaning of a family. My family sustains the minimum definition. No superlatives can be attached. No higher values were involved. I was an accident of biology. My parents did not make me. The act of intercourse resulted in conception. They were not my parents; they were my mother and father in the strictest biological terms.

Later in life when asked questions about my family or family history, I simply stated, "I was hatched from an egg," often confusing those who, for want of a different reason, felt compelled to inquire.

My father, an alcoholic addicted to barbiturates, did not hold a job long enough to keep the creditors away. He came from a good background. My grandfather, on my father's side, earned a PhD from Harvard and taught at the finer universities. My grandmother earned a Bachelor of Arts degree and a graduate degree from Vassar and Radcliff. She worked in fashion at the better department stores. In her spare time, she wrote titillating romance stories under a pen name. She was a crusader for reform causes, including clear packaging of bacon so that producers could not hide the quality of the pork. My father did not graduate from college; he saw no reason to pursue a higher education since he could work any con: at best, he was a grifter. My father was tall, dark, and handsome and could charm the pants off anyone—anyone but me, that is.

My mother, in her youth, was a beauty. Prior to marrying my father, she was a *Vogue* model. She was a beautiful brunette woman—with a body like Madonna. My parents met in Miami Beach, where my father was an emcee at a hotel. Later, he got my mother a job as a cigarette girl. When she was pregnant with me, she stopped working.

I was the oldest of five children—born in Miami Beach, Florida, barely nine months after my parents' marriage. I often wondered if my conception was for the sole purpose of abuse and profit. Now I know it was for both. Nothing about my family was normal. We moved every nine to twelve months. Awakened in the middle of the night, I was told to pack. There was no time to say good-bye; I convinced myself it did not matter, as I had no friends. I went to a different school every year. I never accumulated many cherished possessions, so packing was easy. However, I never got used to seeing my mother on her hands and knees, wrapping her few precious belongings in tablecloths. Like hobos, we were always on the run: one step ahead of the sheriff and the repo man.

With the money he made, my father bought drugs and alcohol. We were inevitably poor. He was constantly drunk and smelled like alcohol. My father walked around the house naked with a hard-on. I once made the mistake of asking a classmate to my house—which was a disaster. I never got over the embarrassment. Our potential friendship was replaced by uncomfortable silence. I knew that this was not how the rest of the world lived. It was certainly not what I saw on TV.

My Family

There was an air of sheer terror and violence that attached itself to our poorly crafted dwelling. This emanated throughout the house; it was palpable: the smell, the taste, the essence of it. Early on, I conceded that my life was to live through the atrocities I was routinely subjected to. I coped by disassociating from my body. My mind went somewhere else; I felt as if I were having an out-of-body experience. The older I became, the more punishment I received for crying and screaming. The punishment was as horrific as the rapes and sodomies themselves.

My younger brothers and sister—forced to watch—were traumatized. As a result, by the age of nine, my sister and brothers turned to heroin to cope. After a while, my sister and brothers did not want to associate with me. I believe they thought that if they came anywhere near me, they might become the target of my father's proclivities. If it had not been for my grandparents (who finally figured out what was happening to me), I would not have escaped the incessant nightmare at the age of thirteen. Shortly thereafter, my grandmother contracted Valley Fever, forcing me into a private foster home.

Laughed at by my siblings and schoolmates, I felt like a freak of nature. When unlocked from the closet and allowed to attend school, I understood that I was different from everyone else. The poverty showed. I possessed two hand-me-down dresses; these were the only two dresses I owned and wore throughout my two years of junior high school. In my adolescent years, I had acne like craters and scars on my face. I somehow survived the torment of my peers. Cursed or otherwise, I was bright. My peers used me to do their homework and copied from my exams. Once my classmates had cheated off my examinations, they had no further use for me—with the exception of being the butt of every possible joke.

For all of my pain and suffering, God never forgot about me. I do not know where my God was through the years of unbearable and relentless pain. Obviously, God had more pressing and important matters. However, I know He was there for me when, one night, I was left for dead. Through twists of fate and by the miracle of grace, I did survive—even through high school when the treatments from my peers were at their cruelest and when my father was the most demented.

The real damage of the abuse and torture showed up later in my life. The commissions of my father's crimes were instrumental in what later became my lifelong journey. I had to work through my life in an effort to make sense of my world gone mad and to have a life different from any medical or psychiatric statistic. The abuse rippled inward as well: a faint echo, never to fully retreat. After I left home, a tsunami of memories crashed on top of me, threatening to drown me—the wash of which led to major panic attacks, where my flight-or-fight response was stuck for indefinite periods. I thought for sure that I was experiencing a heart attack: I could barely breathe, and my chest constricted. After I left home, my father never touched me again. Strangely enough, it was then that I began to feel the pain. Even though he was dead, he inflicted blows on me daily. My father started a deadly and cruel process. As an instrument of torture, my life became a march straight into Hell. As a father, his betrayal of me left irreparable damage. As a moth to a flame, my relationships with men were a psychologically preordained dance—choreographed to end in pain. Each dance became much worse than before. The bed: it was my undoing—my destruction. This became my battleground. The bed was where I waged my wars.

God help those who attached themselves to me and failed to see they were dancing with a tornado or grasped the disclaimer I always made a point of relaying: "I am a piece of work. I come by it righteously." I knew that in all fairness to others, some type of warning was necessary. Some men took my statement of fact as a question to be answered at a later time. Feeling secure, most men believed themselves to be capable of making up their own minds. After I conveyed who I was, I often had to explain: this was not a question but rather a declaratory statement. What can be said of those who failed to take heed?

WHY DO WE FEEL SO UNCOMFORTABLE WITH THIS STORY?

There is no easy way to write about childhood sexual abuse. Any discussion explores uncomfortable truths that society prefers to turn a blind eye to. This is especially true in my case: where the horrors are documented in such a graphic fashion that the acts become tangible. No right-minded person can stomach the horror of these events. It is clearly too much. Fact: it was too much for me as well. There are blind spots in even the most well-intentioned individuals. The failure to see a small child suffer so egregiously is to deny the realities of life. These horrific abuses happened and will continue to play out in the underbelly of life's happenstance if we do not fully grasp the fragilities of a small child and the independent struggle in coming to terms with his or her reality. A child, for example, in an attempt to assimilate his or her own body parts, wonders if the anus is a place where waste passes or if it is a place where people insert objects designed to hurt him or her.

Your mind wants to conclude that, for those damaged children, it is impossible for them to construct lives filled with love and productivity; yet, it is possible to struggle heroically against great odds, to deal with the horrors, and to seek something better for themselves and others. Individuals that deny evil live in a fugue state. Dietrich Bonhoeffer, a German Protestant theologian and anti-Nazi activist said, "The test of the morality of a society is what it does for its children." Today, there are laws that are legislatively mandated for certain professionals to come forward. Why do we have to legislate something decent people should do anyway? Human nature, if left alone, will walk away from something so despicable. It is real, and people survive—but not without consequences. Society has a moral imperative to step forward to prevent sexual abuse.

When sexual abuse is not so rampant, it will stop happening to others like me. That little girl inside of me was frightened by life and the judgments made by others for something so completely out of her control. Yet, she found the courage to wake up every morning and show up for life even when those individuals responsible for damaging her were not held accountable by any standard.

That little girl is Mary Elizabeth; it is I, and I found my voice. When there is justice for all and an accountability of our treatment of others—in *all* interactions—others like me will not have to scream. Society must step up to the plate.

Part of the proceeds of this book will be used for abused children so that they may heal, know a better life, help society focus on better methods of prevention, and establish tighter controls where there are less system failures in an effort to abort horrors for the innocent and unprotected. I want to thank you individually and collectively for being part of this important endeavor.

AN UNPRECEDENTED WAR ZONE

My father's favorite morning sport was raping me—all the while knowing that I would be unable to walk or sit that day. My life took a turn for the worse once we moved from Florida to Arizona. My father's drug and alcohol abuses increased and became entrenched in his personality. Among his other addictions, he was a sex addict.

My father stopped working after we arrived in Phoenix. His speech slurred; he reeked of alcohol and body odor. He sweated buckets. My father, a wild psychopath, was a raging, mean, cruel, and nasty SOB when he was drunk. His breakfast consisted of orange juice with vodka and a fist full of narcotics. He watched me as he consumed his liquid breakfast. His eyes darted back and forth, anticipating any attempt I made to escape. I ran out the door before he could grab me and force me to stay. On those mornings when I could not escape, he forced me to be alone with him. He knew I would flee, so he physically grabbed me by the hair and hauled me into his locked closet. He further sealed any attempt I made to flee by an outside lock he placed on the master bedroom door. The closet was small; there was no light; and worst of all, it smelled just like him: nasty, dirty, filthy, and disgusting.

What I am about to convey was an everyday occurrence for me. After everyone left the house, he came back to the closet, violently grabbed my hair—shaking my body with all his might—and smacked his fists into my head until I fell to my knees. He yanked at my head and stuffed it between his legs, yelling all the while that I was a worthless cunt; his whore; unworthy of love, respect or decency; and not even worthy of being born—his sick and twisted idea of foreplay. His fists hit me against the side of my head; then, he grabbed whatever was handy—the telephone, a lamp, or even a side table—to hit the top of my head. Never fortunate enough to pass out, I saw stars, and my vision blurred. Finally, he beat me into doing most anything to stay conscious and alive, where I had no choice but to take his cock in my mouth. He masturbated until he came—all the while grunting and groaning like an animal until he nearly choked me. I could not breathe as he held my head so tightly against his fat stomach, choking me on his cum while his hands strangled me at the neck. My small mouth could not hold all his piss or cum. He slapped my face because I could not swallow it all. My inability and unwillingness to swallow anything and everything that came from each of his orifices enraged him. He laughed like a mad man, while he continued to shit and piss on me—often demanding that I lick him clean. I gagged and vomited all over him and then vomited again until there was nothing left but the dry heaves. His next act was always the same: he threw me on to the bed, spread my little legs as far as he could, pinned me to the bed, and vacillated between fucking me in the vagina and my ass. He pleasured himself with the show of such a hard-on when he could shove his cock into all my orifices. He was very hard, and I was very little and dry. Every time he fucked me in the vagina or in the ass, it was excruciatingly painful. He actually laughed when he ripped my anus or tore my vagina to accommodate him sexually and with whatever objects he chose to insert. No small child is built to endure what he did to me.

He attempted to kill my spirit by yelling and referring to me as the vilest of expletives: always unworthy, meant only to serve him. This went on for hours until he was ready to pass out. At that point, he kicked me off the bed to the floor, leaving me naked in a pool of my own blood, my clothes ripped and stained with blood, smelling of his shit and piss. I shivered and whimpered like a hurt animal. After curling up in the fetal position—still smelling of his excrement, his piss in my hair and on my face, my body bloodied and wounded—I cried and cried. No one heard me. When he began to snore, I found the strength to crawl toward my clothes and push the bedroom door open, making my way to the bathroom, where I locked the door. The shower was never hot enough to scald my skin and remove every vile and evil remnant. My head hurt; my body felt broken. As soon as my little legs stopped shaking, I grabbed my clothes and left the house—reeling and sobbing.

Sadly, not one person ever stopped to ask if I was in trouble or in need of help or to chastise me for being truant from school. I was invisible because no one wanted to see me. After a while, I grew tired of walking; my legs hurt from all the twisted machinations of my body. I could not sit or stand; I was in so much pain. I wanted to sneak back into the house and find a safe place to sleep. Sometimes, I was fortunate to arrive home in time to climb into the pantry, locking the door behind me. Other times, I was not so fortunate: he would grab me and start his reign of terror all over again. Things got really ugly when I tried to fight and escape from his clutches, because I would invariably fall down or trip. This was when he grabbed me harder and started all over again with a dose of torture as his extreme pleasure. Another round of hell played itself out. How could I survive this all over again in a matter of hours, all in the same day? I knew someday it would escalate even more, and I would not survive; no one could.

MOTELS ALONG THE WAY

Later, my father became a traveling salesman—always on the con. He insisted that I accompany him on his many road trips. We never stayed in nice places—anything that was clean or well-tended. I never had my own bed. My father went out a lot. I earnestly prayed that he would not come back.

Sometimes, I can still see myself in those dirty rooms—red motel vacancy signs flashing in the window through the night: I am huddled on the floor, lying sideways underneath the bed, trying to make myself small and invisible to their clutches. I am scared, tired, hungry, and cold. People always come back to the room with him, bringing foreign and terrifying objects. It looks as if the grown-ups are on their way to a Halloween party. Some of the objects I recognize through the windows—such as a small but thick tree trunks or shovels—others I do not recognize until later. They might just appear to be gardening tools, but I know better. These are tools of torture. There is no place for me to hide—no other doorway to escape from. I am dead; only, I am not dead.

When he brought these men and women into the motel room, he did to them what he did to me next—but only worse. I hated to hear the grunt-like noises that sounded like wild hogs. I knew it was only a matter of time before he came after me with the gang gathered around, waiting for their turn.

Three adults at one time on a small child's body was sick and depraved—an unbelievable horror and shame. The pain was indescribable. If I cried, if I could not hold back my screams, or if I begged, my father would ensure punishments I personally knew I could not withstand. Torture: for a man like my father, torture was just one of many humiliating and degrading acts. There was nothing he would not do or have others do to beat me into submission.

Torture was a concept I was fully aware of since the age of six. His ultimate way of hurting me for not being cooperative was putting his cigarette or cigar out on my small round breasts. As more people joined in, they would follow his lead. I often wondered if the whole purpose of these out-of-town motel trips was to make money off of me, offering me up to the highest bidders and their own perversities. I always feared that was the real reason for all of this. Today, I still have those scars—scars I will never be able to get rid of. Just the smell of searing flesh makes me throw up. That always led to further torture with knives. It pleasured him to cut me in places where no one else would see. This was not the worst of what he did to me, but it is all I can share now without becoming violently ill myself.

In the end, he took me to motels where people do things they cannot otherwise do in the light of day: where no one would know the depth and depravity of his actions. In the end, there was no sexual act I had not performed. By the age of nine, I was a first-class whore.

BOUNDARIES

My earliest memory begins at the age of three: my father fondled me and sucked my genitals while he changed my clothes. By the time I was six, he raped and sodomized me. The other children were forced to watch—wherever, whenever he raped me. He made me fuck the family dog. The violence was physical as well as sexual. When I did not cooperate, I suffered painful punishment. Locked in the closet without food or water or light, I had no idea when he would come for me. Once, when I was six, I was incapable of swallowing his cum. He punished me by taking me to the farthest part of the backyard, where a swamp was filled in with dirt—a breeding area for rattlesnakes—and tied me to a palm tree. He left me there overnight. No one came looking for me at dinnertime or thereafter.

Sometime after that, my family would leave for brief two - or three-day trips. The only problem was that they left me at home—well, not really at home, but outside with my security blanket and a baby bottle filled with water. I always ended up sitting on our neighbors' porch until they returned from work. Upon seeing me, my neighbor was shocked to learn that my family had gone on a trip, leaving me behind. They had no alternative but to take me into their home. Frightened that they would be like all of the other adults I had come to know, I hardly slept at night. When my family returned, my neighbor marched over to my parents' house and demanded to know how they could not have noticed my absence after a few hours—let alone three days or so. My father was non-responsive and just grabbed me and threw me into the house. The neighbor had to realize something was wrong, but as my father had expected, no one wanted to get involved. This was precisely the same reason he did it a few more times.

In first grade, my teacher thought I suffered from a mental disability. I was always afraid. I did not play with the other children, and I did not speak—in fear of retribution. Every day, the teacher asked a different student to pass out the art supplies. It was a joke to others, as they always passed me up. I sat for one hour without supplies—too fearful to speak up. My clothes were ripped apart and stained with dark blood. My teacher and others must have thought that ripped and stained clothes were the result of poverty. If a hole in the earth had opened up, I would have climbed into it, dragging the dirt behind me. My teacher became concerned when, after a week or two of class, I had not turned in any drawings. When she confronted me, I was scared into silence. That is when my teacher called the school doctor and nurse and told them she did not believe I had the maturity or possessed the requisite intelligence for the first grade. She explained to the school's doctor and nurse that maybe next year my parents could try to enroll me again. After multiple examinations by the school's medical professionals, they saw no reason to hold me back a grade because of my intelligence level but were more concerned about the way I sat and walked. They spoke to my mother about this because they thought I might have spinal issues that needed to be addressed. If they had only known why I could not walk or sit, perhaps I could have received intervention. Terrified to talk to anyone, especially grown-ups—I knew better than telling them—I returned to class with the proviso that I speak up when not given the necessary art or writing supplies. Sometimes, I still look back at those earlier times. I wonder: if given a chance just how far I might have excelled?

My father convinced people that I was an animal. Out of five children, I was the only child taken out in a harness. In addition, I was forced to have an enema before going out so I would not have to bother them with asking to go to the bathroom—in fear that someone might notice something and finally act on it. It was always about controlling me—every bodily function. I was the oldest; yet, I was the only one forced to have an enema before leaving the house. I once got sick and vomited in a department store on a sale table of sweaters. I got the hell beat out of me right then and there—in front of numerous witnesses. Not one person spoke up. Instead, they watched the beating as if I deserved everything I got.

My family—all but me—usually ate what was cooked for dinner. My father made me hamburgers from Skippy dog food. In a tension-filled dining room, I sat down with everyone else. My father forced me to eat these horrible Skippy dog food hamburgers every night. The disgusting warmed-up dog food made me gag, and invariably, I vomited almost immediately. My father would not allow me to leave the dining room until I ate every bit of throw up. Every evening was the same. I was always the last to leave the table. Later, I would ask myself: what type of sicko does this to a small child?

As a child, I was grateful not to be questioned about my family. In retrospect, I probably sent out signals that I did not want to be asked. People sensed when to remain silent, and if nothing else, I deflected their interest. I never realized that I had manipulated them into not probing for information that I would rather keep to myself. Conditioned not to tell or ask for anything, I feared the punishment my father would inflict and the pain I could no longer bear. The timbre of my voice alone always revealed the entire range of my soul; one needed to hear only a single word to know whether I felt strong, weak, tired, passionate, or angry. Much like anything else in life, I grew up to understand the significance of this fact and made my plans accordingly.

Childhood is supposed to be the time for bonding with your parents—a time of nurturing, nourishment, and growth. My childhood was a time of brutality, cruelty, and control. I was so confused about where my body ended and my father's began.

A TEMPORARY RESPITE

Every Sunday, my grandparents came for dinner. On one Sunday night, everyone was there for dinner: the five children, my parents, and my grandparents. My father had taken so many drugs with his martinis that he collapsed face-first into his bowl of chicken noodle soup. He was inhaling the broth, noodles hanging from his nostrils. As often witnessed in seriously dysfunctional families, everyone else sat at the table as if nothing happened: sipping their soup. Every gut instinct I had was screaming for a grown-up to act like one and push his face out of the soup bowl. After dinner, my grandparents simply said to me, "Pack a bag. You are coming with us." I did not really understand. When we got into the car, my grandmother turned to me and said, "There are two things you will never talk about: what your father did to you—and money."

So, when I was thirteen, my paternal grandparents took me away. They were retired and lived in Phoenix. At my grandparents' house, I was loved, adored, and cherished; there was nothing for me to fear. I had three regular meals a day—the same food my grandparents ate. My grandmother sensed my pain, and when looking into my eyes, she saw a horror that only she seemed to understand. Somehow, she knew I needed to be loved and held. She also knew I desperately needed a playful distraction. I remember her telling me that she needed to walk across the street; she had a surprise for me. She brought back a McCall's magazine, which had a section for children to cut out paper dolls and their clothes—something I never experienced before. I played for hours on end, successfully distracted from any painful thoughts. I loved and adored my grandparents with all my heart. I am very much like my grandmother—as you will come to see. That is an admission I am proud to make.

Six months later, my grandmother contracted Valley Fever, and for health reasons, she needed to move away from the desert. My grandparents moved back to Florida. I was unable to go with them because my grandmother was so sick. They placed me in a private foster home—a good one. They made sure of that. It was a Catholic family, and the father was a bank president. I lived there until I left for college—with the exception of a six-week period of time when my foster father was ill, and I had no other options but to return home. . .

ADOLESCENCE

Teenagers, for the most part, have a hellish time. In an effort to fit in, the child—an adult in the making—must buy and wear the right clothes, be a part of the right social group, and come from affluent neighborhoods and the right family. To move through adolescence relatively unscathed, an adolescent needs to possess status and certain material possessions which grant him or her the look of the privileged and popular.

My adolescence was an absolute terror. I stacked the furniture against the door and slept right after school before my father returned home. I did my homework late at night or toward dawn. One night, during the six week period I returned from my foster family, my father broke into my front bedroom window, bringing with him one of my classmates who lived down the street. When I went to bed that night, I thought I was safe. My furniture, moved against the wall, barricaded me from my father's attempts to come through my door in the dark of night. I was wrong: my father and classmate broke in through the front window.

Together, they raped me. I wished they were dead. Had I found a broken glass with razor-sharp edges, I would have killed them both. I crawled out of bed to hide underneath my dresser. I wished I were dead. I knew I could never again go to school—my last and only refuge. Now, I had been marked. My senior year was less than two weeks away, and I would be the butt of a joke that would never end. My school assignments were subsequently sent to the house.

Since I was not attending school, I applied for a job at a very small diner named "Orange Julius," which served hamburgers and chili hot dogs and the famous Orange Julius drink. The small diner was on the same path my brothers and sister walked on their way home from school. I made certain they knew the days I worked so they could always count on me for dinner. Every morning, the owner came in to count the hamburger and hot dog rolls. When he would find six or seven missing rolls, he inevitably asked me if I ate all the food. I detested lying, but I told a whopper when I looked into his eyes and admitted to eating everything in sight. As an anorexic, I never ate; yet, telling my boss I ate everything that was unaccounted for was a lie I had to tell to ensure that my brothers and sister ate. I put what tip money I received each day into the cash register to make up the difference. I saved my paychecks for college; occasionally, I bought groceries to send home with the kids.

One day, my brother Edward, already a heroin addict, brought a friend to the house; both were stoned out of their minds. I was not working that day, and I went to the store and bought hamburger meat for my younger brothers and sister. My brother began making two very large hamburgers for himself and his friend. I said, "Edward, do not use that meat; I am cooking dinner for the kids." He pretended as if he did not hear me. I told him to stop on two more occasions, the last of which I said, "Edward, if you do not stop, I will force you to leave that meat alone." They heard me that time and laughed hysterically. On a challenge "to make them stop," I swung my fist and hit my brother squarely in the jaw, cold-cocking him to the kitchen floor. The laughter stopped. I was horrified by my sheer outburst of rage and the violence I aimed at my brother. He was becoming more like my father every day. I knew I embarrassed him, and I felt terrible about hitting my brother. Yet, I was the designated caretaker of my younger brothers and sister by default; I was the mother of the house: always cleaning, washing, and ironing. God forbid there was something out of place when my father arrived home. I was a desperate young woman: no childhood for me—my life skipped straight into adulthood almost from the first time he touched me. It was a childhood that could never be recaptured after he stained me with every vile part of his body.

My father was so drunk that he and my brother were always setting the kitchen on fire. On one occasion, my father, suffering from a drug-induced brain, took it upon himself to cook a ham. On the face of it, one could concluded it was a fatherly gesture to make sure his family ate—until you realized he forgot to place a pan beneath the ham. In his stupor he placed the ham directly on the oven rack. The ham caught on fire, then the stove, and eventually the kitchen curtains. I learned early on how to put out kitchen fires. This happened more often than you might think—with my brother and father so stoned and drunk they simply did not care what happened to the house or whether they set the kitchen on fire. Life was very unpredictable for me as there was always one disaster or another just around the corner.

Even though I could not attend school during my senior year, I graduated near the top of my class. I was surprised; it felt so wonderful to be selected as a recipient of awards and acknowledged by Sears and other large companies for my grades and accomplishments. It was truly an amazing feat for me since I lived in a war zone for most of my life. My high school had a special luncheon, prepared by the parents, for the recipients of scholarships. The tables were beautifully set with white tablecloths and real cloth napkins and adorned with gorgeous flower arrangements. Every place setting had a card designating where the scholarship recipient and their respective parents sat—each parent was set at the side of his or her child. This was a horrifying moment for me as my parents never showed up. You would think I would have been used to the rejection and complete abandonment by now, that I would have anticipated it. I did not think the situation would be this bad. The table was overflowing with happy students and proud parents. Granted, I received scholarships and honors. Dumbfounded by the obvious lack of my parents' presence at this ceremony, I prayed they would remember and come later. Later never came. I was struck by terror when I thought, *Oh, God—this is another sick joke on me.*

I often felt that if I were perfect enough, the chaos surrounding me would stop. My parents should have embraced, honored, and surrounded me with love for all of my hard work and achievements. I felt that I could never be perfect enough—even when other families would say what a wonderful young lady I was: so bright and always helpful. It was then that I knew there was nothing I could do to change my parents' minds about me. I just did not count; perhaps I was unworthy. I only saw that I was worthless; after all, parents are supposed to be there to protect you, watch over you, and take pride in your accomplishments. I was not worth the bare minimum of respect or care from them. My embarrassment and humiliation prevented me from looking up at the counselors and guest presenters or looking around at all of the very happy people. I wanted to share in their joy and success. This was a joyous occasion—meant to be a celebratory and memorable event for all. When the presenters called my name, I received applause from other parents and students, but my wobbling legs were barely able to stand to accept my hard-earned prize. I know what others must have thought about me and the empty chairs surrounding me; their collective pity was unbearable.

I became interested in Catholicism early in my adolescence. In my house, there was such chaos and unpredictability—an absurd and abject disorder of reality—that hyper-vigilance was the only way you survived. In the Catholic Church, I found order out of chaos; the rules were well-defined—something I desperately needed. There, I found peace and an inner quiet. In my house, nothing was ever spelled out, and everyone was always at risk from my father's uncontrollable rage. Discovering Catholicism and the spiritual path to self-enlightenment became a life-altering event for me.

I applied to the University of San Diego in my junior year of high school. It was, at the time, a college for women and run by the nuns of the Sacred Heart. I wrote them an eleven-page letter about my life and aspirations, asking for a scholarship. I was so excited when they accepted me with all of the scholarships and financial aid needed to live in the dorms and to apply myself full-time to my studies. Later, I was informed that this small private college for women wanted me so much that I was the very first student ever to be admitted on financial aid. I wanted to be a novitiate—in preparation for taking the vows of religious life. However, in my first year at USD, I got in trouble for smoking Marlboros and drinking Ripple with the seminarians. I became pregnant from a young man—not my boyfriend at the time. There were my sexual appetites.... The convent did not remotely appear to be my destination.

DOES THE STORY EVER END?

The answer is clearly *no*; it never ends. Bad memories need no triggers—they just are. What happened to me as I was growing up was an atrocity. Words are inadequate to discuss feelings and reactions to a child so abused when they are far too overwhelming—especially when constricted by the alphabet. At times, my writing seems disjointed. I sound child-like in relaying the brutality. It is not the dispassionate writing of a professional. It is the grown woman that writes about her responses, and it is the professional that analyzes and summarizes the consequences. I am certainly not a multiple personality. That which appears disjointed is the observable remnant of childhood sexual abuse.

Childhood development is hallmarked by the quest for self-identity. My father was not the silent sentinel to my adolescence; he was a predator of the worst kind: a monster masquerading as a human being and, even worse, as a father. My childhood, capped at both ends by trauma, shame, and loss, was lost to me forever. My innocence was destroyed; my childhood, annihilated.

I lost my sense of self. It was a soul-shattering moment when I realized that a woman's self-concept was rooted in the eyes of her father. Self-loathing singed my soul. The complete unfairness of this distortion was outrageous. There have been more than a few desolate times of impenetrable darkness and despair.

Judging Me

For a child of abuse, there is a terrible feeling of shame, guilt, and disgust; but there is also enormous physical stimulation. A young child can feel far before it can tell right from wrong. It knows pleasure and pain, comfort and discomfort. The young victim of abuse feels both. The abuser knows how to manipulate the combination; it is his or her form of control. It is only as one grows older that things do not feel quite right.

As a child, I knew acceptance and self-consciousness. I discovered my rebellious streak much later.

I always sensed the anger in my father: waiting to hit me like lightning bolt—a wicked thunderstorm a brew. As an aspect of his control, he wanted me hurt. His goal was to destroy my spirit. It was impossible for him to destroy my soul. When a person experiences extreme pain, especially associated with the trauma of terrible sexual abuse, there is a natural psychological tendency to dissociate. Most people take their mind to a pleasant place: to good family memories, a sunrise, or a field of flowers. I had no good memories where retreat was possible. (Even today, I have not one single memory of something good or tender from my parents.) Instead, I dreamed about what I would become.

The consequences, however, were very much in the present. As an adolescent, I had a severe case of anorexia, and I was a self-mutilator. I weighed as little as seventy-five pounds in high school. With food, I could control what went into my body and what did not. With self-mutilation, I could control my pain and my reaction to it. I created my own pain to focus on—inflicted on the outside of my body instead of the other pain that was eating at me from the inside. Yet, there was nothing rational to my response. Self-mutilation and anorexia often occur together and are expressions of self-loathing—an internalization of the abuse I suffered from my father. This was accompanied by a desperate need to hide the shameful ritual from others—just as the evidence of my sexual, physical, and emotional abuse had to be hidden in silence.

For a victim of abuse, the impulse toward destructive behavior is overwhelming. It tends to override anything else that might be going on.

Only later, in my twenties, did my reaction come out in anger, rebellion, and revenge. I learned the lesson my father taught all too well: sex is power; it is life and death. So I chose one-night stands—never looking back.

When my father died, much later in my life, I did not feel very much. I had spent years wishing him dead, but I knew that my anger had not killed him. I wrote him an impassioned letter about how much I hated everything he had done to me and placed it in his coffin. I attended his funeral, but I did not mourn him. Instead, I mourned the father I wished I would have had. My mother died some years later; I could not go to her funeral. It is a regret I have to live with for the rest of my life. I have specifically chosen not to write about my mother. This is out of respect for my nieces and nephews who have good memories of her as she was a different woman when my father was no longer a part of her life.

I became numb over time. The internalization of my trauma followed me into adulthood. This left me confused. My erratic behavior and the secrets, rituals, guilt, shame, and self-loathing left my personal life in chaos and uncertainty. These emotions played out throughout the developmental period of adulthood: most commonly reflected in my relationships with the men I later chose. Throughout adulthood, the one lasting trait was my inability to trust. My late husband, a psychiatrist, analyzed me well when he stated, "You will never give it all to one man." I simply noted it and looked out the window. Hearing his words spoken with great certainty, I knew he was right. Much like a stockbroker, I learned to diversify my portfolio in an effort to minimize any emotional risks, dividing my needs between all of the men in my life; every base was covered where others stood in line.

People want to know how a person learns to deal with all of the horror. We learn to deal or life ceases as we circle the drain waiting for the body to catch up after the soul expires. Suppression of life's traumas works for others as easily as denial until later in life, when faced with some inconsistencies of childhood memories, they become conflicted over what really happened and what memories were buried alive. A disease referred to as Alzheimer is a medical condition usually observed in the elderly. I understand the medical definition of this disease; however, philosophically, it is the ultimate brain shutdown of what may have been a painful life. This concept does not at first blush seem to be so far off as the severely injured body shuts down by going into shock. I have often wondered—since it is not inconceivable—that some people (who suffer more traumas in this world than others) may at some point just shut down.

Survival requires a different skill set. To thrive is the ultimate goal. Yes, I dealt with what happened to me—but how well? Externally, surgery could minimize the scars of childhood abuse; in the end, I just had to go on. We all do what we have to do to move forward. Unfortunately, many abused children decide to repeat the patterns of abuse into adulthood: the abused may become the abuser; the abused seek addictions; or the abused continue to repeat the pattern of victimization. Pain is so familiar to someone who has been abused—that is all they know. Any other emotion just feels too weird.

Many do not understand the power of redemption, new beginnings, or second chances. Emotionally, this was how I moved forward. I was an innocent child, yet I embraced a life of guilt for many years. I repeatedly asked, "What could I have possibly done as a child to deserve this—all of it?" Through visualization, a metamorphic transformation occurred in my life. Through reflection, revelation, and celebratory reveling, I prepared my soul for new adventures and for continued growth. An awareness of my unraveling began at an early stage in life. Perhaps, finding a single loose thread could lead me to where and how this all began, and my work to undo the damage could begin. The discomfiture of this process allowed me to find a spiritualism that has sustained me and brought me to newer heights of consciousness. A harsh reality check—a dissection of sorts at the various times in my life when I wanted to blame something or someone outside of me for my faults—was a painful but necessary part of growth. Learning to find my weaknesses and addressing them without rationalizations was grim. Finally, coming to terms with where my own boundaries were and where other people's boundaries lay was a lifelong search and an enormous challenge. Driven to seek good over evil, I became a well-honed warrior.

My sense of humor saved me from going insane. It is said that it takes a village to raise a child; but for those of us who have no one but ourselves to really rely on, we must go through a series of steps, sometimes repeating the entire process until progress is apparent. At that point, redemption occurs. Real growth is hard work, harsh, and sometimes humiliating. Humbleness is the key to self-authenticity. It opens new doors we could not have otherwise walked through and opportunities we never would have seen. Not one of us can afford to give up on growing; growth is essential to a long and productive life. The opposite of no growth is stagnation—a dishonorable death when we have come as far as this on our own. Life may at times fool us into thinking we are not alone. Yet all of us are born alone and die alone. Martin Luther King reminded us that our lives are lived between the dashes on our headstones. We are born, and we shall die. What matters is what we do with our lives in between the dashes. We are held accountable for gifts and aptitudes given to us and for climbing out of depressed valleys, regardless of whether someone placed us there or we got there all by ourselves. It is more important what we do after the valley—our strength of commitment to staying out of the valley, the healing we seek, and the new beginnings we make based on second chances—because we have discovered, after all is said and done, that we are more worthy than we thought. We can seek and find a meaningful life. It is this lifelong lesson that we share with others that makes all of the difference between where we came from and who we are today.

This chapter would be incomplete without some thought as to whether forgiveness of my father for his monstrous deeds is a prerequisite for healing. Some so-called experts (who, by the way, have not suffered such atrocities) state that healing cannot commence without forgiving the perpetrator. I view this differently. I will never forget what happened. In healing, I have learned to place less significance on the abuse. The crimes committed against me do not control my everyday activities or decisions—at least, not very much. My everyday dreams control my life. I feel that I am worthy of a future—a future of my own making. God will judge. How can a mere mortal forgive a monster—a psychopath without a conscience or an ounce of moral fiber? It is not up to me. Good and evil are conjoined at the heart of all human beings. Whether nature or nurture controls is not for me to speculate. It is a far more complicated issue than I am equipped to figure out. The journey is life long, and I am not opposed to revisiting this matter. It is a certainty that a heart cannot both hate and love simultaneously without creating spiritual blockages that hinder progress.

I do not harbor hate but rather love: love for life, family, friends, and myself. Everyone's set of circumstances is unique. It is a choice made by the individual. Whether forgiveness is essential for you to move on is a personal decision. Hate, however, is not a healthy option. Moving on and giving the abuse lesser power is a healthy option. I do not feel a compelling sense of urgency to make any decisions about forgiving my father. I am a very spiritual person, but I am conflicted. I do not view such a monster as a human being. There is uncharted territory that I have yet to confront. The journey is ongoing. When—and if—I am confronted with whether my healing would be more complete or is dependent on forgiving my father, I will deal with it then. I am healing; I have moved forward. I have made a life for myself that anyone would be proud of, that is good and whole. The fact that I feel worthy of a future speaks volumes in itself. I no longer view my self-concept through the eyes of my father but rather through my own eyes.

I believe that the progress in your life will dictate whether you have to come to terms with forgiving the perpetrator. You will know what to do and make your choices accordingly.

A VISIONARY

Dissociation is the distancing of self from a current reality: a real-time denial of any connection or involvement with somebody or something else. Dissociation is a coping mechanism that children often learn when they are brutalized. It is a natural coping mechanism when the body has exceeded its ability to deal with the physical and mental pain. We all dissociate to some extent or another. Babies do it quite regularly. It is a natural, physiological response to being overwhelmed. The sexually abused child is extraordinarily overwhelmed. Dissociation allows the sexually abused child to literally take a break from the pain—to distance himself or herself from the horror of what is going on and ultimately survive. The process can be explained in many ways, but for me, it was an out-of-body experience where I watched from a distance what my father and others did. The horror and the pain were still just as real to me.

I can state with certainty that, throughout my childhood, there were no pleasant memories for me to retreat to for solace and comfort. Strangely enough, all I had within me was my belief in tomorrow. I began to plan for my future—but not just for the short term. Dissociation had its purposes: to stay alive and sane. How I implemented my plans for whom and what I wanted to be became a forerunner for what later turned out to be one of my greatest abilities: visualization.

Judging Me

For ten-plus years, this was how I survived the brutalities. I survived through imagery—by an ability to think of a world so very different from the one I saw and experienced every day.

I dreamt of a world where there were no monsters ready to eat you at nightfall—hiding under your bed or in the closet. Rather, it was a world filled with good people: kind and loving people on the street corner, in the malt shops, at the drugstore, and more importantly, in your own home—a mother and father like Ozzie and Harriet or Lucy and Ricky, people who watched over their children and cuddled and hugged them close for being such precious miracles. The loud cheers coming from the park were for the children as the parents watched and clapped as their child slid swiftly down the slide—fearless and with the greatest of ease. I imagined a world full of smiles and laughter. And as I thought about this new world just outside my door, I gave great thought as to what my place in that world would look like. I knew an education was tantamount to all new beginnings. I wondered how much school would be required of me to be that person, which schools I would attend, and what I would come home to. I wanted children of my own and to make wonderful cakes with clowns climbing up the sides or a merry-go-round of horses—especially chocolate cupcakes with seven-minute frosting.

I watched *Perry Mason* on television, where justice was accomplished in one-hour increments. I wanted to be a judge. Television judges were wise and compassionate and knew so much about the world. These judges did not appear mean or cruel; they did not raise their voices, and they never hit children or took them to scary rooms where the child never returned or where they were bloodied and beaten upon when they did. My father told me that only the rich and politically connected could be judges—not someone like me: viewed by my father and others as poor and stupid with tattered and bloodied clothes. I never let on that this vision was

A Visionary

mine and mine alone: a secret I did not have to share—not with him or anyone else. The secret was between God and me. This had a freeing effect on me, and I began to feel free. Visualization left me with a whisper of hope as if a feather had brushed against my check.

In real time, I was never more abused. I began to see a sliver of light at the end of what was once a dark and dank hole. I never lost sight of my precious dreams. My mind played my visualizations over and over again until one day that person sitting behind the bench presiding over hearings and the woman at the park with her children—always smiling and laughing—was me. I saw myself. I became exactly who and what I had envisioned all those many years ago. I had finally arrived.

A broken and damaged child—brutalized beyond recognition—can envision a life so unlike the one she experienced as a child. To envision something better for one's self is the foundation for becoming a visionary. This child was me: later to become a very well-known federal civil rights judge with two beautiful children who laughed, loved life, and loved each other.

I later came to learn that when you make a plan, break it down into doable tasks, and focus and refocus, the goal comes to fruition. I embraced my visions, and they saved my life. Visualization was the single most powerful personal tool in my arsenal. The reality I envisioned was mine; it was my life, and I made it from scratch—just like my seven-minute frosting.

All of us are visionaries whether we know it or not. I am now blind; does this mean I cannot visualize my life as I want it to turn out or who I want to be? I cannot see with my eyes; yet, an absence of sight does not exclude me in any way from dreaming and reaching for the moon.

Judging Me

We have the power to create our own world, and we have an equal amount of power to destroy it. Throughout the day, choices are made; each of these choices moves us away from our visions or serves to enhance the probabilities of making them come true: one building block set upon another. Some of us feel we are not capable of visualization. Believe me when I tell you that it is possible to make gold out of straw. Whoever told you it was impossible to be anything else other than a repeat of your perpetrator was absolutely wrong. Even under the worst of circumstances—much like the concentration camps—no one can take away our ability to think and control what truly belongs to each of us—our minds. Suspend disbelief. Settling for less than you deserve is not an option.

Most of us think of visionaries as someone with a very high IQ: those who live in a rarified atmosphere of academia or think tanks, worlds away from the average person. We think a visionary is one of those precious few individuals who were born with creative or intellectual aptitudes.

The truth is much different. When I dream about my future—pray for a different tomorrow, promise to conquer old fears, release old pain, overcome new challenges, and find new strengths—I am a visionary. For those of us enlightened enough to understand the concept of *"getting out of our own way,"* we begin to see the world with fresh, new eyes. Adamantly adhere to the strongest of your commitments.

Bad things happen to good people. Diagnosed with multiple sclerosis and systemic lupus in my late thirties, I was so mad at God that I refused to speak to Him. A friend purchased a book on healing through positive thinking. For the first time, I surprised myself by throwing the book right back at him and with enormous bitterness and sarcasm stated, "You think positive; God and I are not speaking." To make matters worse, well-meaning people told me: "God would not give you more than you could handle." I bitterly laughed in their faces. I wept. I begged and pleaded with God; I had not signed up for this. Wasn't it enough that I was so grossly violated as a child; that I lost my husband very tragically; my brother murdered; that I suffered a battle with cancer; and that I buried the most important people in my life? I begged the question, "What did I do in my last life to deserve all of this?"

Every time I vacuumed, cleaned the toilets, washed my dishes, scrubbed my floors, or dusted the furniture, I could not stop thinking about God. Unfortunately, God picked those moments to try to get through to me. Had He forgotten we were not speaking? Well, I, for one, had not forgotten. I did not want to hear anything He had to say to me. I was beyond furious. If He started to talk to me, I ran into the bathroom and flushed the toilet twenty-two times or fifty times—or whatever it took to drown out His voice.

"Why do some people have all the luck while my life turned to shit?" This was the time I finally accepted that life was not fair: Humpty Dumpty did not fall; he was pushed. There was no "Prince Charming"—just a bunch of toads. And underneath all that shit I figuratively and literally shoveled, there was never, ever, going to be a pony! I was inconsolable.

One thing I have discovered is that I never did anything to deserve what happened to me. That issue is resolved. Why bad things happen to good people is something we will never know. What I do know is that we are gifted with an opportunity to rise above our fate and do something extraordinary with our lives. I would not be the same person today had I not lived through those terrible moments. I will never know who I would have become; I only know who I am today. That is all any of us will ever know.

Judging Me

One glorious day, I woke up and felt a lightness in the air; the sun was radiant, and the air felt like butter. My heart was light; the heaviness disappeared. I finally accepted my reality. I had multiple sclerosis and systemic lupus. I was losing my eyesight. Whatever would happen, for better or worse, would happen. My future remained uncertain. I really do not know when, how, or where my heart transcended my fears. I had previously arrived at the point where I understood everything intellectually, but until my heart accepted the truth of these new challenges, I was out of my mind with grief and hopelessness. On this very morning, I woke with the knowledge of a heart that embraced my new reality and was all the lighter for it.

I, for one, am grateful that vision has precious little to do with sight but lives in our minds. I am thankful that I know and understand the difference. For those of us who are disillusioned, dispossessed, or disenfranchised and without a whisper of hope, there is now the possibility of an expanded set of options. A total awareness of opportunities and advantages opens the gates of our minds to envision what we want our world to look like and who we want to be and decide what steps are necessary to fashion that reality.

When you acknowledge and embrace your reality as your own, you move forward. Regardless, follow your dream. What awaits you there is beyond anything you could ever conceive of.

Once we own our reality, we are free. We can become anyone we decide to be—to reach for the moon and hold a star or two. It matters not where we came from; it only matters what we are going to be today, taking with us all of the necessary measures to make that vision a reality. We can cast aside all negativity and those outdated self-limitations. Nowhere are our names attached to the old self-limiting baggage we have been carrying for what must have been an eternity. We collectively kicked it to the curb. I, for one, think it is time to celebrate ourselves and to smell the roses.

Your self-worth is now intrinsically linked to the visions you conceive. The key is to dream large, and when other people's reactions to you attempt to make you feel small, smile; you are in the big leagues now. Be vigilant and aware of opportunities and possibilities that you never thought about—let alone, heard of—as they are knocking at your door. This is your second chance. They brought friends, life forces you never met, and realms of joy you never experienced. No longer will either of us have thoughts of an inadequate self.

The self-actualizations of your visions are forming as I write. You need not flesh your visions out in their entirety because visions are defined as you grow. Slowly, your visions are self-actualized by your choices; these choices are manifested as actions that must be in the same vein as what you envisioned. There are two types of choices in life: life-enhancing or life-diminishing. If you begin to apply this philosophy to every decision you make—regardless of whether it's personal or professional—you will find that amazing opportunities will make themselves known to you. You, the incredible you, are now standing at my door waiting to tell me so much more about yourself and your journey! I can hardly wait to hear your story, to stand in your radiant glory, and to see the glow of pure light shining from within you.

When you come into my house, you will see words written in lipstick on the bathroom mirrors. At first blush, you might believe you have just entered a crime scene. I assure you: that is not true. This is how I stay in touch with my visions. I find a mantra—a prayer, a dream, or a sentence—that reminds me of life-affirming choices that are magical and inspirational and that keep me focused forward. A sacred mantra works best with constant repetition throughout the day, always when I feel scared or overwhelmed by life, and, especially, when I am discouraged.

These are my prayers before I sleep and the words I breathe every morning when I awake. Later, the prayers turn from the general to the specific; it happens during those unusual and unexpected moments of life. For me, when I am inspired by another person, a song, or a work of art, my dreams become more concrete, and my visions become more specific.

If each of us can establish a daily ritual with the repetition of our own mantra, the impossible now becomes possible, and the world is truly ours for the asking. It is only by thinking large that we accomplish our dreams. When we act abundantly, we manifest those visions into abundance. Consciously, we move forward: each word we speak and each step we take never in conflict or in negativity with what we envision for ourselves.

May all of us dream the dreams that actualize our visions into realities.

THE DEVIL MADE ME DO IT

For many years, I tried to understand what drove or compelled me to suffer. The searing pain erupted without much notice on my end. I blamed it on the men I later chose. After all, there had to be an outside actor to keep me imprisoned in such deep pain. I would have done anything to blame my despicable behavior with the men in my life on something or someone outside myself.

Adam and Eve, from the well-known biblical story, lived in paradise, wanting for nothing. What was the draw to the apple? After all, Adam and Eve were blissfully unaware of the apple's juicy flavor. What was so compelling about the apple?

At what point in the spiritual continuum does humankind abdicate or surrender its free will? Have we intellectualized the question beyond understanding with layers of very convoluted and complex theories so that we no longer ask the question? Just because something is difficult to seek out does not mean the answer is not worth the search.

No one is perfect—a fact most all of us would agree on. The imperfections in each of us are born from early life experiences, before we even understand the events themselves. Logically, it must be these early events that pierce our armor and inevitably allow the devil to slip in. For me, it was so predictable that the tall, dark, and dangerously handsome man across the room would be the face of my devil. As magnets, we were drawn to one another—I, with the neon sign on my forehead that read, "For a good time, call...but only if you are unavailable." He was everything I feared: he was my father all over again. Beguilingly, he was breathtaking—an apparition and a curse; I, awestruck. He was not your devil but mine. If that were true, then the devil appeared to each of us differently.

The next logical conclusion is that each of us was born to a unique hell of our own fashioning. In the instant case, my hell was right here on earth. From a distance, others only saw a very handsome couple; no one had any idea that a drama as old as time was being played out. I, needing to go back in time to make my past right, and he—God only knew. This is why we seek, search, and journey for the answer for why we do what we do. In addition, it is also why no singular book, lecturer, or way is the key.

We are born as miracles: armor intact. Once the placenta is ripped away, we stand naked to the brutalities of life—without armor. This is how the development of the cracks and crevices—the deterioration of the soul—begins. Exposure to the harsh realities of life is extremely high; the damage is done. It is in the damage that our vulnerabilities form: where his "come hither" look is so devastating to me that he is as hypnotic as hell.

The formation of the cracks and crevices depends on the exposures we have to life and the type of protection offered to the young. I had no protection; thus, it is easy to see why the devil comes to me in the forms he does: tall, dark, dangerously handsome, and a real charmer. The games begin. He's never a prince of a man—just another toad in the road. The devil himself is hardly recognizable as he or she bears many faces; for each of us, the devil is custom-crafted. When the cracks and crevices break open, the foundation weakens. The solution is to be hyper-vigilant: to guard against the incessant rendering and tearing of our souls. It began for me when I was only three years old.

There are no signposts or markings for the potholes or crevices ahead. We just fall into the abyss when we take our eyes from the spiritual pathway. Actually, it is no different from texting while driving in traffic. If we take our eyes off the road for an instant, we are swept away into some calamity of sorts. (The vibes aimed squarely at me by Mr. Unavailable were nearly unbreakable.) The act of free will is not the falling but in choosing instead to take our eyes off the road even for a momentary glance. It is the path to no return.

This is when I catch his eyes clearly focused on me: ablaze with something indefinable but seductive. It is very difficult to pull back from his radar; the magnetism midflight, the seduction sets in quickly. The defining moment is in taking my eyes off the road and gazing for a second too long into those deep, chocolate-brown eyes. Those lush and long black lashes find me falling headlong within this man's spell—the black hole. Even intellectually understanding the dynamics at play, he magnetizes me with a vector-like force from which I cannot pull away. The devil's machinations are actually far more seductive than they appear. Here is where we freely abandon our free will because we lack the necessary spiritual discipline required to return to the road less traveled. The hyper-glance so necessary to remain vigilant for the Christ-like path is momentarily stripped away. It only takes a second to surrender to the noxious fumes and poisonous gases. It is a trap for the unwary. It is definitely more than a state of mind; there is an enormous chemical attraction, which is addictive like heroin. Sometimes, we move through life on automatic pilot, and *oops*: there goes the unconscious slip—his smile that makes my knees weak, like puppies' breath or jelly doughnuts. The ride to the center of the universe is the highest of highs and the lowest of lows—always destined to end in pain. The curves in the road are very dangerous indeed.

Judging Me

The path to our Higher Power is different for all of us. We do not get credit for our aptitudes. Aptitudes are God-given talents; the goal is to develop the talent into the highest of human endeavors. I have learned that the spiritual path of goodness is a challenge. We humanly disassemble. The cracks and crevices, once realized, exposed, and made known to us, measure our weaknesses and strengths. If we are truly ready to meet the struggle between good and evil, we need to do so with the necessary mental musculature and the spiritual discipline to walk away from the devil or fall prey. The concept of this reality is not so difficult to understand. Sadly, it is in the implementation of our goals that the key falls away from the lock.

It is said that the character of a person's soul is made known by the dialogues that are kept with God. If my life were truly going to change for the better—if I wanted to overcome my own innate destructive tendencies—I needed to perform a thorough postmortem of my soul. It was not a pretty picture. The autopsy was harsh. To get at the very truth of who and what I was necessitated a complete and total exposure of my underbelly in the full light of day.

To examine a piece of tapestry from the backside is to see a confusing assortment of threads woven in a chaotic pattern. For some of us, there is a need to understand where we stand when naked to the realities of life—stripped of all defenses and gross rationalizations. Once I started the process, I had no choice but to place every aspect of my life on a cold, sterile metal table—scales stationed above me—and weigh in every conceivable part that was undeniably me. When the process was completed, I compared myself and my life to a norm: a range of numbers manipulated and tweaked at the end of the day by psychobabble experts that tell us "we aren't so bad after all,"—the "I'm okay; you're okay" mentality. I decided against the latter based upon what appeared to be a shit-load of excuses, and I examined the raw scores in the light of day. I wanted to know the very depth and breadth of my blind spots, weaknesses, and failures. I did. It was a grossly time-consuming, energy-depleting, and depressing experience that became so overwhelmingly painful that I had to rest only to begin again. Some people feel self-reflection is self-indulgent, but I feared self-delusion even more.

Although my intellect fully absorbed the results, it took my heart much longer to incorporate the atrocities of my soul. When I came this far, the realities of the pain, disgust, and shame could not be denied. I feared looking at myself in the mirror or looking at others directly in the eye. It took a great deal of time and courage to heal from this process.

In summary, I had no regrets for exposing what should have been known to me a long time ago. Real growth was now possible for me. Once again, there was no one to blame but myself for my own stupidities, my choices, and the suffering and pain I inflicted on myself. No one else was responsible for me but me. The realities of my life—and what and why I did what I did—shattered my soul. I could now see why I waited until I was fifty years of age to take on the horrendous task of my soul's postmortem. Even then, I had not developed the necessary mental musculature to be strong enough to grapple with the corruption of who I was.

STUCK IN THE MOMENT

"Who in the world am I?
Ah, that's the greatest puzzle."

—Lewis Carroll

After all was said and done, you would think by now that I had a full grasp of who and what I was. Oh, I knew exactly who I was not, and I was fully aware of the crimes of my body and heart. So what was the problem? I was the problem; I am always the problem. I knew my life was less than it should be; there was so much inside me that stayed shut down. It hurt so much to know I was not living my life to its fullest. My energies were so suppressed, and my talents and abilities were not being utilized to their fullest potential. I held myself in this illusionary prison. As a prisoner, I could not break free—no matter how hard I tried. I was trapped in a prison of my own making.

Early on, there were plenty of warning signs that my life was out of balance. I was severely depressed; my life was depressing. Granted, at times I had good reason to be depressed, but it was not so much that I could barely function—the talk of a consummate overachiever, no doubt. I was not just stuck in the moment, I was stuck—period. My life seemed disjointed. I wanted to believe that

I had inadvertently stepped into someone else's nightmare and could not awaken this person to let me go. I went to law school; I received an MBA; I was an elected official, held a mayoral appointment, and one of the top ten teachers nine years running—so why was my life like some pathetic reality show? I never signed up for the life of an abused child. Is it any wonder my life was filled with such an absurd, abject disorder?

One day in the doctor's office, I found a very old *Cosmopolitan* magazine that contained an article on depression followed by a self-help quiz. I asked myself the following questions: *Did I need the latest, best-selling antidepressants?* Answer: No, I was already taking the maximum dosages allowable under FDA regulations. *Did I need a new job, need to change my hair color, need to cut my hair, or need to move to another city?* Answer: No, I had recently just done all of the above.

It had to be a bigger issue than *Cosmopolitan* was willing to address. I knew in my gut it was a deeper and far more serious problem than I could wrap my mind around. I recall that in speaking to my daughter, I told her I needed an attitude adjustment—an understatement even by my own standards. My ever-so-bright and wonderful daughter remarked: "Get real, Mom; you need attitude surgery—and stat!" This was not, however, a particularly new revelation to her or to me. The tragedy lay in the fact that I could not seem to do anything about it. I was literally stuck in the moment—a moment that grew to a week, then a month, and then several months; life was simply overwhelming me. The situation had come to a critical mass. I needed help, and it was not the type so readily available in the yellow pages.

I continued to pray to God in an effort to get unstuck. I believed that life was a series of lessons learned. Perhaps somehow, and in some way, the answer was too obtuse. Yet, I kept thinking as I watched and studied other people functioning in their everyday life that they were moving forward, and I was left further and further behind. "Why?" I asked. "Am I really that dense?" This was very serious: not even retail therapy worked, and up to this point in my life, at least shopping managed to soothe the weary beast—even if only for a moment.

Fact: I knew I had to be really screwed up. If this was my truth, then I had to find a way to unscrew myself—but how? Where was this so-called instruction booklet on the workings of a human being where I simply could look up "stuck" in the index? What about those of us who came from a dysfunctional family with steamer-trunk baggage and who never learned how to cope with life on any level? It was for people like you and me—people who really needed to find answers to questions that most people deal with on an everyday basis—that I wanted to find the answers. Individuals that came from fairly balanced homes carried "fanny-pack baggage," and for the most part, they were highly functioning people. It is a universal truth that no family is perfect. There is a degree of screwed-up where fanny-pack baggage is the minimal degree of discomfort and tolerance. No doubt, the sexually abused child grows up to carry steamer trunk baggage. In my house, anger was handled by sheer unmitigated violence. You were lucky if you didn't get your head blown off or hit with the butt of a gun. I often wanted to ask other people how they managed even through hard times. What did they do about all of their pent-up rage? They did not appear to be in the middle of a crisis, but everyone at some time or another *is* in crisis—aren't they? However, asking this of a perfect stranger sounded ridiculous. With my luck, the question itself would have me declared as certifiably insane. That was not an option. So there I was—back to square one.

Then it hit me: the only viable solution might be to get my happy ass back into therapy. *Ugh!* Therapy is work—hard work. If you decide that you want to consult with a therapist and you want the experience to be productive, you must work *with* your doctor. In other words, be honest with yourself and your therapist. It is only then that you can begin the real work of healing. All of us could benefit from talking to a professional at one time or another. Some people have endearing friends who can listen and offer helpful insight. For me, this involved trust to a degree that not only would exacerbate my problem but invariably would become *the* problem. Initially, I saw this as a worthless endeavor.

Opting for therapy with a trained professional guarantees some level of trust—but not entirely. A patient must do his or her part in the discovery of the why, and then the healing process can begin. Lying to your doctor is very transparent because they *get* a lie, and if going forward was indeed what you wanted, lying is completely unacceptable. The shrink will know: very seldom can you fool a doctor into believing a lie. The pure beauty in talking to another person whom you can trust, and who, by oath and as a therapist, will not violate that trust is reassuring to those of us who trust no one. The well-informed doctor gathers some early assumptions and works with you to develop a well-opined analysis. Ideas can be postulated or formulated when the facts of your background are revealed and can actually lead you through a decent rehabilitation and ultimately to the solution of your dilemma. A step-by-step description of how and what happened leads to a win-win situation. Life is hard. Then, life happens to you, and the test along your journey is how you measured up to the challenge. Life's journey is a process by which you change what you think and transform who you are. It is a lifestyle decision that is not for the faint of heart. At times, you need the help of others to transition through.

Some doctors are good about helping others figure out their lives. I can say it helped me. Even more surprising to me was that it actually worked. I needed a major tune-up: not the small routine oil-and-filter change. In peeling the same onion all over again, the concepts were more deeply understood. Thank God, I was not stuck anymore. Admittedly, it was a close call for everyone involved.

> "The road to success is not straight. There is a curve called *Failure*, a loop called *Confusion*, speed bumps called *Friends*, red lights called *Enemies*, caution lights called *Family*. You will have flats called *Jobs*. But, if you have a spare called *Determination*, an engine called *Perseverance*, insurance called *Faith*, a driver called *Jesus*, you will make it to a place called *Success!*"
>
> —Author Unknown

METAMORPHOSIS

Metamorphosis refers to a magical transformation. The transformation is best noted by marked changes in appearance, character, function, or condition. Biologically, the alteration is characterized by a change in form and habits during the developmental period following the embryonic stage. One who studies the developmental stages of human growth defines metamorphosis as the complete transformation of a fertilized egg to an adult human. This is similar to the change of a tadpole into a frog or of a caterpillar to a butterfly. It is the alteration of one thing into another. It appears as if something magical has occurred. In truth, it is at once both mysterious and magical. This is what makes each of us such wondrous and unique creatures. In humankind, the process of transfiguration is observable, it is the development of ourselves into our true, unmet potential. As humans, we uniquely have the opportunity to witness our lives unfolding. As we continue to develop, we open, embrace, expand, and enhance our own higher consciousness.

Granted, there are times when the process is aborted for reasons we do not always understand. The process in people is often stymied by an individual's refusal to change. Change is traumatic. Generally, people abhor change as it is disruptive and challenges the balance within the constructs of the human brain. As a result, people prefer status quo—to be with the devil they know as opposed to the devil they do not. No growth—or being stagnant—is a death all its own. Chaos develops during the changing process. During the growth process, our center shifts about until the process of change is complete. Left behind to suffer a tortuous death are those individuals stagnating in their own closed-mindedness as new truths surface daily and new scientific studies demonstrate the need for changes in almost every area of life.

We cannot change our lives if we do not own them. If we have convinced ourselves that we are fine the way we are, we will never seek to change and better ourselves. Those who selectively refuse to acknowledge what they know to be true about themselves and what others have so often pointed out—much to their consternation—are only fooling themselves: not others. Who wants to continue getting the same results from doing the same thing over and over again? This is why many people revert to drugs of choice, work, alcohol, narcotics, and sex—the whole gamut of addictions—to avoid the pain of reality. The call of the question is where does the pain come from, and why does this pain paralyze us and cause us to be dysfunctional? Silence and solitude are deadly to those who suffer from denial; this is why those opposed to change stick their heads in the sand. We understand why a child is afraid of the dark, but it is truly a tragedy when an adult is afraid of the light of day.

However, solitude and silence helped me connect with my soul—my inner being. Without self-reflection, we could never move forward to self-actualization. My serious postmortems, however brutal, became life-enhancing, never life-diminishing. I learned at an early age that life never calmed down long enough for me to wait for tomorrow to start living the life I wanted today. Indeed, I wanted my life to begin now. Periods of silence allowed me to open up and see my life with all of its ugliness, fragilities, and gross acts of intentional conduct where I sought revenge for what my father did to me. All of us have kinks in our wiring—some more than others. These kinks cause the growth process in the metamorphic stage to short circuit, retarding the potential for full development. The points where I personally blew a fuse brought about paralysis. Solitude allowed me to be honest with myself in my genuine search for who I was and allowed me to systematically discover ways to change the areas of my life that were not working on any level. When we run amok, we know it. The void of constant noise and action may seem scary at first because there are no distractions from reality. Silence can be deafening as well—but only to those who fear the truth.

When I initially examined my own hardwiring, I saw it through a protective body of water. After my first attempt at studying what appeared to be nothing short of a god-awful mess, I experienced a meltdown and immediately shut down. I experienced the worst kind of fear. Nothing made sense to me; too much had transpired in my life already. My brain misfired. It was a lot to absorb. I felt as if I were experiencing computer problems. All sorts of files opened and closed—unprovoked by me—along with red flashing system-failure messages. I started to speak in non sequiturs. My thoughts collided, cancelling each other out.

Fear bored a hole through my subconscious. Without fear, I never would have forced myself to take a longer and closer examination. The inculcation of my education at least put me on notice that something had gone awry. Finally, I peered through the water and saw what appeared to be a puzzle. I discovered noticeable shapes or forms in the wiring. Some of the tangled messes had beginnings and endings. I thought: *What would be the harm if I worked on one mess at a time?* It took a long time for me to feel comfortable with this idea. Thus, it took time to work out the tangled wires. Why? Because there were so many messes. Change would have been virtually impossible without deep self-reflection. Time is a precious resource that we habitually waste because we have deceived ourselves into thinking we have so much of it to spare. Not true: life can and does turn on a dime. We do *not* have all of the time in the world to figure out what is working in our life and what needs changing. It is a lifelong process which must begin in the now if we ever intend to make much progress.

Going deeper and deeper within the murky waters of what is revealed to you through the developmental periods of growth becomes much clearer as the murky waters of life settle. Unfortunately, when the waters tilt—i.e., messing up your life even more—it causes the rivers that flow within to become murky. This makes it so much harder to figure out exactly what problems remain hidden from sight. After periods of silence, the water clears, and you can see straight to the bottom. The periods of silence are crucial to rewiring your soul. Solitude permits the wires to unwind and take shape so that they are manageable to grasp and rewire as the river calms.

Finding the center of your being is the hardest part of all. First, the center is forever shifting on you as you change. Initially, your center shifts dramatically; however, the more time spent in the examination of your soul, the deeper the struggles become to unwind the tangled mess. The mess you made has to be cleaned, and your center has to be shifted. It is not a new place that you hope to arrive at but rather an augmentation process—a paradigm shift—so necessary in an effort to reset your wiring. After a while, the shifting will not feel so disorienting because there is a certain peace that follows the shift to the center. The resulting changes—the source of peace—are not moving away from the tangled wires but moving toward the center of the wiring. If you are just barely able to distinguish one mess from another, you have made progress. It is true: changes occur so rapidly that the waters become murkier and unreadable. It is terrifying until you see that there are opportunities even in the middle of chaos. If you are dedicated to change, you do not turn way from what appear to be new adventures. It is your body and soul's response to change that separates the child from the adult. Courage will sustain you—even if you remain unaware that your courage manifested itself directly from what has been developing in you all along. The reality of change alone is horrifying because it is uncharted. At first, you can only observe what you believe to be the message, as it is earth-shattering. You, and only you, can determine whether the message is part of your truth.

During moments of uncertainty, which are many, I maintain a very close relationship to my Higher Power. To believe that I can change without help from a Power greater than myself is insanity. If I capitulate into the thought process of being able to do this on my own, I am undeniably nuts. What good can possibly come from a vacuum? The waters will remain murky, and the disorientation of life to reality will be upside down forever.

The inertia alone will kill you. Therefore, have the strength to will your life to change until your Higher Power stabilizes you. Most likely, the changes in life do not come about in your time, but in His time. It is a given: praise, prayer, and an abundance of gratitude for the ordinary and sacred within your life will bring about the most extraordinary help when you least expect it. It is grace that brings amazing insights to you from the most unexpected avenues that enlighten you beyond measure.

A constant dialogue with your Higher Power always serves the journey of change. There is strength in admitting that you cannot process all of this on your own. This straightforward admission helps you to become a better person. The more uncomfortable you are with your changes, the more time you have to contribute to others. Make your life about helping those who need you. No matter how disoriented you feel or how far off center you shift, helping others calms the waters.

Discipline and vigilance are the tools you will keep with you to get through the rougher times. They are necessary to do the mental work of purifying the heart. Always keep in mind that the ego is sly and insidious. Coming into your best self is the hardest work you will ever do—but the single most rewarding. At the heart of life, your journey of change and how you accomplish it are the only things in life that ultimately matter.

If I want my life to work, I must be diligent and disciplined. The excuse bank is always full of reasons to step aside. Rationalization is the ego's slickest trick. When I fail to care about the process or tire of the fight, bad things almost inevitably arise. This is because I have given up on my Higher Power and myself. You will know when the process is aborted.

At times, I feel weary and conflicted. I am so easily distracted by my own weaknesses. When I am lazy, I slide backward. It is easy to lose sight of the goal. At times, I feel fragmented and disjointed and fall into despair.

When this happens, you begin to spiral down a deep and dark tunnel without a place for your feet to find purchase. In climbing back up and out of the hole, we fear someone is waiting at the top to kick our fingers off the ledge. It will take every ounce of strength you can muster to hold on. With your Higher Power, you will be back on solid footing. Now, you are all the stronger for the test. You will know when it happens. No matter what, get back up and begin where you left off—even if you ended up two steps backward. This is a lifelong process. Every day, life's realities change and morph into other challenges that you must be prepared to encounter. Believe me when I say to you that just when you think it cannot get much worse, there is an obstacle of monstrous proportion waiting for you: your next challenge. Only with the help of your Higher Power can you continue to go on in life's journey, ready for the unexpected. Challenges will become second nature to you, and so will the inevitable struggle to thrive. Soon, you will begin to help others, leading by example. It is a very humbling experience when others come to you for advice and guidance. The humbling comes from the very realization that you have come the distance.

It is at this point that an inward journey to examine your own progress is a good reality test. A friend once relayed to me during one of my darkest hours that change was possible when handled in increments of inches. She went on to poetically state, "Yard by yard is far too hard." I found this concept to be credible. Nothing as important as change can be rushed without a thorough examination of one's heart and soul. Moreover, even then, you must look at each angle in the transformation process and hold it in the light of day, turning it repeatedly to see how it fits—if it fits—into your life. I remember that in my prayers, I repeatedly asked that God not to be too obtuse when answering my prayers as I seemed to have an ability to overlook the most obvious.

Change for me took a very long time; I had a lot of growing to do. At first, it appeared as if life took far more from me than it gave. I was so confused at times that the natural course of revenge upon the men I later met seemed as normal a concept as any other I could have imagined. As it turned out, the only person hurt during these frequent vengeful episodes was I, as the men I chose were indifferent to any message of revenge I attempted to convey. So, I asked, who were the losers and winners in this scenario? The truth to this question is now easy to see; I was the loser—and only I. Had I not had the courage to develop from the childhood violence perpetrated upon me through a deep-seated need to seek revenge from men in the name of my honor, I would not be the person I am today. I am a far different woman—I hope, a better woman—on my own spiritual path. Metamorphosis, upon the transformation (however chaotic and frightening), is no different from a birthing and a complete renewal of self. Not one of us can be as cavalier as to brush off our deep-seated imperfections that we so blindly use to hurt others—regardless of our intentions.

THIRVING THROUGH CRISES TAKES MONUMENTAL COURAGE

It took me nearly thirty years to survive an early life of injustices, abuse, betrayal, and deceit. It was the refining fire (the testing of my mettle) that honed my skill set and sharpened my purpose. I am driven by the very potent belief in my own competence and by the determination to win for those who are disenfranchised, disillusioned and dispossessed.

It is no longer enough to simply survive life's horrific tragedies and absurdities that attempt to define us. I was a survivalist for thirty years. It was not enough for me. As humankind, we must strive for a higher goal. Regardless of what life dishes out, the ultimate goal is to thrive. How does a person thrive who has lived through the worst he or she can imagine?

First, he or she fiercely holds on to whatever sanity keeps that individual from running headlong into ongoing traffic. Eventually—and when ready—the abused works through the multiple and painful steps of grief analysis. This is the second step. Once that is completed, one now survives. This is a hard process and requires bearing down upon pain that is mind-blowing. It is a very lonely journey. Each person who passes through this process is a survivor of his or her own personal holocaust. Much is to be commended for surviving through a journey of hell. Sometimes, we want this state of existence to be good enough. After all, no one can begin to understand what it is like to be us as we are going through all of this. It is hell on earth: a form of purgatory all its own. Initially we must accept life on its own terms: to skip this process while attempting to survive is a form of denial. Once we arrive at the state of survival it is imperative that we understand that simply accepting life on its own terms is no longer enough. So what are the options? Do we opt to stay here, or do we move? We can move one of two ways—going backward after lifting ourselves from the vortex of hell is not an option. We are left with going forward, but we have to ask: what does going forward look like? Although, we are not certain; we are cautious. Sometimes failures mount up. Just when we think we are really going to lose it, a light shines. We become committed to an idea that is pregnant with possibilities. This is similar to a mother who lost her daughter to a drunk driver and becomes an avid spokesperson for Mothers Against Drunk Driving. She seeks and finds a filial duty to a worthy cause and honors that commitment.

There is a quantum leap between surviving and thriving. To thrive is the ultimate paradigm shift—a shift that many are unable to maneuver. The difference between surviving and thriving is an attitude: a mindset that embraces something better because we believe in doing more than surviving. The bridge is to behold a filial duty to a worthy cause and an honor to that commitment. Now the paradigm has shifted.

I celebrate you for the courage it took to survive. Yet, I personally want something more for you. I want you to thrive. Thriving is lifting yourself above what life has dealt out. In doing so, we accept that it will not bring a daughter back or erase what happened to you as a child. In embracing the necessity of thriving the abused takes back his or her personal power. Honoring that commitment usually begins with the determination to serve others who have lost their way. This is not making lemonade from lemons or even chicken soup from chicken feathers; rather, it is making gold from straw. Unfortunately, we do not get the opportunity to change the past. If we are very brave, we make something from the debris—words I do not use lightly.

When danger or the chances of a severe outcome are an abstract concept, it is easy to be fearless and unafraid. Whether a person decides to fight or crumble when faced with a present danger or threat to his or her equilibrium depends upon that person's courage and psychic energy to rise above. We have a personal choice under these circumstances. As individuals, we select how we will face life and whether we survive or thrive.

It is not about what to do now; rather, it is about whom we decide to be. To be is a higher state of mind. Many survivors go the route of "doing" to prove themselves worthy to themselves and the world around them. Their value is measured according to the length of their resume: If I have accomplished all of this—whatever *this* is—then I am worthy to myself and to society. This is a cycle that never ends; it comes from the old adage: "What have you done lately?" At what point do we declare that enough is enough? At what point have we done everything to show ourselves and those around us that we are worthy and desirable? If it is about doing rather than being, then we are the hamster that goes around and around on the wheel without a destination certain. At some point, we must determine when to stop proving to ourselves and others that we are lovable. We were always lovable, desirable, and worthy. We just did not know it. We never had to be all of those line items on our resumes.

I have suffered more than my fair share of major depressive episodes: through some of the most tragic events in my life, I shut down. Unconsciously, I wanted someone to take control. I wanted someone to restore a semblance of order to my life, which suddenly and without warning was pitched into total chaos. Everyone else except me was going about his or her routine. People went about unscathed and unconcerned when my life felt like it was in total ruin. I often resented their complete disregard for my personal tragedy.

Those who know me are aware that after every blow, I turned to work—my drug of choice. There was always an edge to me; now I was just edgier for most people's taste. I know that during these periods, I spiraled down into a deep, dark vortex of frantic, frenetic activity in perpetual motion. I stopped being a human being. I stopped seeing friends. I did not go out, and I did not have people over. I stopped exercising. I saw nothing that went on around me. I no longer had the ability to feel. I was numb. Food had no taste. I never noticed the weather. I was sensory deprived. Somehow, through it all, I made no mistakes in my practice. If anything, I became more obsessive. However, my absenteeism as a human being was detrimental to my children; in the office I was not a good boss, and it began to show. For sure, I was a lousy friend to everyone I knew.

This is what I am referring to as the chance to take control of our attitudes and make choices that enhance our lives. Once spiraling down into that deep dark vortex, I could have been lost forever. It was not what I did at this point but the attitude I embraced that saved me.

Survival is merely "satisficing" in life: managing to get by—the state of a *C* student. In the face of a real threat to our integral selves, we make a choice to either satisfice or embrace an attitude that binds us to a worthy cause. That we are loyal and honor that commitment makes us capable of thriving through horrific and absurd circumstances.

In essence, it is not what we *do* in life that counts; instead, it is what we *need to be*. It is the state and the manifestation of our reality. Injustice might have originally defined me, but it was my all-consuming attitude to seek justice for others that made all the difference. Through my own periods of serious depressions, I knew the ultimate path was not what I did but with what attitude I chose to lift myself out of the vortex that could have claimed my life. There were times when the distance between my life and no life was so slight it would have taken no effort at all to pull me into the absurd. The only way out for me was to find something to commit to: not something to do; rather, an attitude that I could embrace.

Seeking justice for those who cannot fight for themselves is a pursuit that deeply binds me. My honor to this commitment has allowed me to rise above a set of ongoing horrific and absurd circumstances. Most of us have faced life's inequities and found that those of us who turn to help others are bound *to* one another as opposed to *against*. It is the attitude we embrace in life that counts—not the busyness of doing. This reality is what separates a survivalist from those who thrive. May we all come to thrive—regardless of the circumstances that set us apart. It is in remembering that we cannot change the facts of the past that we consciously decide how to face it, the choices made in doing so, and the belief system that we will embrace for our new reality.

REFLECT, REVEAL, AND REVEL

The three *R*s—Reflect, Reveal, and Revel—are a powerful part of a cyclical and evolutionary process toward humanity's self-enlightenment. Initially, self-reflection is self-knowledge void of criticism and judgment. It is what we intuitively know about ourselves. The process of self-reflection is just the beginning in the necessary order of events. It is the excavation of self with personal acknowledgment for those feelings and eventually leads to an understanding of those feelings. It is only after much reflection that we can reveal to another who we are. To revel is to celebrate the strength and distance of our journey. Reveling is a respite throughout the difficult travails.

Reflection

For most people, the thought of self-reflection is self-wounding. Some people see self-reflection as self-centered. I prefer to reflect upon my truths rather than be tied down by my own self-delusions and madness.

New Year's Day is not the only day for self-reflection or to make promises for change for the upcoming new year. Any day can be the start of new beginnings. When we examine the soul, we open the door for new ways to better our lives. The sooner we journey down the path of self-reflection, the closer we come to our desired goals.

New beginnings require a self-excavation. The premise is that we will truthfully examine our souls. It is an ideal time for personal reflection: to take account of what is working in our lives and what is not. It is time for personal closure and new beginnings. The very realization that we are human beings means we are multifaceted. Multifaceted implies that we are complicated pieces of work that require a heartfelt response from our excavation. It is imperative that upon self-reflection we move forward to the acknowledgment of our feelings. If we do not own our feelings, we will never change them. This process is complex. Many areas of our lives need serious makeovers. A reflection of our financial well-being is tantamount if we aspire to be independent; *how* independent means determining what standard of life we want and how hard we are willing to work to attain that standard. There are many other facets: such as social, physical, emotional, and spiritual. It is a vast exploration of all frontiers and a lot to contemplate. Even if we do not accomplish each of the goals established, self-reflection helps us to understand why.

Self-reflection expresses the capability of humankind to exercise understanding in self-awareness. It is introspective and shows the willingness to learn more about our fundamental truths. It is only one snapshot in time—among many others—where we glimpse our true nature, essence, and purpose. Self-reflection is an on-going process that helps us develop a deeper understanding of the experiences and beliefs that color our future interactions. It is important to remember that we cannot take on too much at once. That is why we fail in our initial resolutions. The first step is the excavation and acknowledgment of our feelings. The second step, the understanding of those feelings, allows us to change past attitudes and unhealthy thoughts. We are then able to work out our feelings in small, manageable ways. The process of self-reflection—excavation, acknowledgment, and understanding—is the true gatekeeper to substantial changes. It is a way to release inner roadblocks and allows us to become aware of the things that hold us back from moving forward. The whole purpose behind self-reflection is self-understanding.

A sexually abused woman lacks confidence in her own skills. She feels isolated. Self-reflection is at once scary and illuminating. She is not secure in her attachments to other human beings and finds self-reflection as further separation from others. She is without external security. The lack of self-confidence causes her to experience discomfort from within her. A host of other issues may or may not surface. Some of these are: poor self-perception, fear, anger, guilt, blame, shame, humiliation, and helplessness. This makes her interior world frightening because her hardwiring is short-circuited. The child is overwhelmed with emotional and physical issues that seem hopelessly impossible to overcome. Self-reflection is the key that begins the wondrous transformation to one's unlimited potential. It is at this stage that there is the opportunity to be a witness to this transformation of one's self. Self-reflection provides the way for the abused to step forward and to face their insecurities and attain clarity of feelings, purpose, and meaning.

Self-reflection is different from visualization. Reflection requires the strength to focus on a lesser state of mind. The fact that it is less than some kind of normal measure simply means that there is less than adequate measurement for the abused woman to survey her soul. As a child develops emotionally, it is important for the child to have balanced feelings. It is critical that she feel worthy to protect herself and to pursue her dreams. Guilt, a debilitating emotion, must be balanced against the so-called crime. Guilt for something she was incapable of defending herself from is a harmful detractor from full self-development. Her world is turned upside down and inside out. Is it any wonder she struggles against herself and others?

I am not certain when I began the process of self-reflection. I knew right from wrong long before the process of self-reflection. This required penance from me. The penance varied, but I was fixated on struggling to make a wrong right. Sometime after that, I began to develop the ability to look back upon an intellectual concept like guilt. It was childlike in the beginning. Based on my own reality, the feelings needed to pass the test intellectually; however, it was not emotionally processed for some time thereafter. The development was stunted because it was so overwhelming.

A sexually abused child keeps his or her own counsel while feelings free-float about. These are clearly not feelings he or she will expose to another simply because they are feelings. This does not mean the child will ignore what feelings are stirred up. Like most feelings or strong-based issues of thought, we need more than a vacuum for further development. Herein lies the problem. The child and the woman cannot trust. This is innately known. Although the initial process is stunted, he or she is a quick learner. Conflict demands resolution. The sexually abused child will sit long and hard on conflict while seeking the answers. When the child feels he or she has accumulated enough data, he or she may or may not move on. Feelings surface whether we want them to or not. It is not as simple as putting the genie back into the bottle once the top has been removed. This is why we often see the very young child, adolescent or the sexually abused adult turn to drugs or other vices in an effort to quell the onslaught of feelings. As the child matures, the process is oftentimes accelerated. Once he or she begins to figure out the rationale for deeper-set issues, the search is advanced toward a resolution.

One of the hardest parts of self-reflection is fear: fear that the child might see something he or she does not want to see. People are afraid of what they do not know. It is the basis for leaving the light on at night. Fear is a very powerful emotion. It has the ability to paralyze. Living in fear is living a life that is thwarted with danger at every turn. I lived in fear most of my life. In my adult life, it transferred over to acts that most people do without giving them great thought. Fear was always my biggest obstacle. I know the bitter taste of fear—the chill it wraps around me and the paralysis that results from not knowing how to walk through it. The first thing I learned about fear is that you must go through it. You cannot conquer fear by going around it or over it. The most the latter can do is simply put it off. This makes dealing with fear that much harder. Fear has a face to me—at least I could sense fear for what it was when it descended on me: "an ice-cold cobra slithering down my spinal column, one vertebra at a time, ready to constrict at a moment's notice." This is a scary picture, but fear is scary too. Fear has a chilling effect that transcends through the bone to the blood and the heart and lungs and, eventually, it winds its way to your brain. I know this because when I have a panic attack, it feels as if I cannot breathe: my heartbeat is very fast, my blood curdles, and my bones weaken. This ultimately leads to paralysis: a period of time when my brain, like a computer, has an all-systems failure alert. I want to run to my bed and pull the sheets up. Anxiety medication can dull the initial pain. However, the reality of fear is the fact that it does no good to numb the feeling. Fear bored a hole through you; only a sober soul can conquer it. Panic attacks make me feel helpless—which escalates my own problems even further.

Judging Me

I despise fear because my brain just will not operate. It is as if a stun gun shut it down for a few moments in time—only later to be revived and feel the ice-cold cobra crushing my ribcage.

Although I have not yet mastered the beast in its totality, I am more readily able to talk some sense into my state of mind. The argument goes like this:

What is the absolute worst (worse than the worst) thing that can come from this experience (the one I am afraid of)?

Answer: *To the best of my ability, the worst-case scenarios are either* x, y, z, *or a combination thereof.*

I ask: *Can I then handle these scenarios?*

The answer is more likely to be *yes* than *no*. If for some reason my immediate response is *no* or *hell to the no*, than further analysis is necessary in an effort to fully understand what I have refused to acknowledge. The goal is to arrive at a *yes* answer: *Yes I can handle that.*

This does not happen overnight; we did not get this way overnight. However old I may be, my neighbors frequently ask if I am up all night, every night. Of course, being as leery as I am of other people, I ask the question, "Why?" They usually state the obvious: "Your lights are on all of the time." "Oh, that," I say. No further information is forthcoming. Why should I have to admit to perfect strangers that I am still afraid of the dark? It sounds ridiculous. At least I know it. I am now down to one lamp and a night-light. Self-reflection: it's better to know what I am dealing with than to have some free-floating anxiety that I cannot pin down. Conquering fear has been a noteworthy experience. Trust me, it still rears its ugly head, constricting and paralyzing when

I least expect it. There are triggers that set off the feelings of fear. As we mature, there are some triggers we are aware of while others blindside us. Today, I know what I am dealing with: make a quick and dirty analysis and head for the goalpost. Struggling into your best self is hard, hard work.

Whenever possible, we should spend time self-reflecting in quiet solitude—without distractions. This allows us to experience a paradigm shift in our consciousness sooner rather than later. It is not a substitution of one thing for another. We will see our progress as an augmentation of life rather than a fractured series of multiple lifetimes. Self-reflection is the very key to moving forward and evaluating where we went wrong the last time. In closing, it is important to convey that when we look upon our mistakes, we should do so with a pure heart. This allows us to wipe away our mistakes with all of their negative attachments, increase our enlightenment, and allow our goodness to shine brilliantly like a polished diamond. Self-reflection allows our state of mind to relax and become calm. It is through self-reflection that we learn about ourselves in the true meaning of the word.

Revealing

Once the abused makes progress through the acts of self-reflection, it is time to decide what to do with all of those feelings. As I stated earlier, no one lives entirely in a vacuum. Revelation is sharing our feelings with another person. Trust or trusting is the abused survivor's biggest dilemma. The abused will trust in one of two ways: he or she will either trust unconditionally where red flags or signals of distrust will have no meaning to his or her fixated and permanent state of trusting too much and far too soon, or the sexually abused will not trust at all—two very opposing extremes.

Trust is a necessary part of any relationship. Oftentimes, there are impediments to these relationships based on the inability to trust. At the root of all trust issues are past betrayals. These betrayals force the betrayed person to think of himself or herself as less desirable than others. The inability to trust is based on several factors, for a person who suffered from childhood sexual abuse is vulnerable and afraid to trust.

One of the factors has to do with a broken creep meter—one that requires more than the simple tune-up. This has everything to do with not knowing whom and how to trust. It is the failure to trust appropriately. Experiencing sexual abuse during the early developmental stage severely impacts the ability to trust in this world. There is a developmental impairment in the ability to judge trustworthiness. The sexually abused were never taught how to look for the red flags given off by the untrustworthy. Ergo: they trust people who are not trustworthy and do not trust those people who are trustworthy.

If he or she trusts unconditionally, no number of red flags will change his or her beliefs. It is a permanent fixed state that is not part of the dynamic growth process. On the other hand, if he or she mistrusts everyone, even the slightest perceived rejection or criticism will deep-freeze any relationship. Thus, the voluntary breakup: I leave before you can.

A child that was abused early on in a familial relationship experienced egregious betrayal at an early age. The betrayal was so fundamental and insidious that being violated by others is an expectation. We usually get what we expect. This is a very vicious cycle. For the abused that trust unconditionally, they purposefully select people who are not trustworthy and are then disappointed in their choices. It is a self-fulfilling prophesy.

This kind of cycle can only be broken when we figure out the kind of qualities that indicate trustworthiness. You must also develop trustworthy qualities within yourself. Self-confidence and faith in who you are must be present before you reach out to others.

The level of self-confidence required is hard to develop in the violated because their roots took purchase on shame, guilt, and fear. The relatively normal person develops his or her self-worth built on the foundation of support and love. As a result, a poor foundation makes it extremely difficult to build the necessary self-confidence.

The violated have a very hard time in differentiating the intentions of others. One must be able to discern and correctly interpret the behavior of others while simultaneously understanding that trust is a process in a dynamic relationship. Moreover, it is difficult to correctly evaluate personal relationships and one's own well-being in connection to those relationships. The inability to correctly evaluate a personal relationship finds the sexually abused survivor defaulting to old beliefs and habits.

When we acknowledge that our internal beliefs are flawed and can hurt just as much as another's betrayal, we begin to seriously consider our old beliefs and habits. Old coping mechanisms are doomed to fail. Giving up old familiar ways of thinking and acting is both difficult and painful. However, it is an essential step toward resolving trust issues.

All humans are born with a fundamental need to love and be loved. When this developmental process is not formed, adult survivors feel a lack of self-worth, that their feelings do not matter, that they lack personal power, and that they are unlovable. With this thought process in play comes the inability to trust others or their own gut instincts or a continuing pattern of trusting the wrong people. It is only by working on trust issues—or the lack thereof—that the person can learn to maintain healthy boundaries while letting other people in.

Only when you are aware of your feelings and set boundaries accordingly can you take full responsibility for your thoughts and actions while the other person does the same. This is a crucial move forward in creating an intimate relationship.

In writing this chapter, I closely examined the history of all my prior relationships as I thought about my own trust issues. Some men I trusted unconditionally; these men were not trustworthy. Trust must be earned over time. Trusting someone who is not trustworthy with your most private and personal feelings approaches dangerous waters. I fooled myself into thinking one man was trustworthy; instead, at that moment, he was a recipe for massive destruction. "Why," I asked, "would he keep a secret so easily used against me?" These types of men do not remotely want to understand you. To believe otherwise is delusional. Their goal is to use and abuse you. With this man, psychological warfare was made more deadly by the secrets I relayed. Their own personal drama gives them permission to be an untrustworthy person.

In the history of my relationships, I witnessed my heart boomerang right back at me in the sickest, most convoluted and mean-spirited ways possible. No, I did not learn my lesson the first, third, or fifth time around. I expected betrayal, and I was betrayed. After so many hurtful and painful disappointments, I retracted my feelings and kept them to myself, using old coping mechanisms as a defense and revenge. I became a mystery even unto myself. Although I acted as if I had self-confidence to spare, the truth was far uglier, for my self-esteem was never lower. I did not trust myself. If I could not trust myself, who else would find me trustworthy?

Reflect, Reveal, and Revel

Learning to trust made me a train wreck. It took me a very long time and happened inadvertently when I met my neighbor Peter. I had no one to advise me to steer away from the fallout and debris. (I do not know how I managed to survive all of this—going from one extreme to the next.) After a while, I took a sabbatical from dating. I enjoyed it so much I did not reengage for some time. Peter and I became friends while I was in this hiatus. When I met him, I was not looking for anyone. I was completely risk-averse. Sometimes, the most unexpected surprises come quietly into our lives.

A life without pain was wonderful. Emotions were still a sticky issue for me. However, it was at this point I began to observe the so-called normal person and how they handled trust issues. I learned more than you can imagine. Individuals with precious little baggage from childhood form close associations to people whom they eventually learn can be trusted. They do so over a period of time and are generally less fearful of betrayal. Trust is not something we give away to just anyone. It is about taking a wealth of life experiences, applying what you know to others, and deciding whether that person is trustworthy. Learning to trust others with just a little bit of your truth to see what happens is just the beginning of the process: do they turn your truths around and use them against you, or do they understand you better and love you even more for sharing? If the answer is the latter, then you have come a long way.

I invariably go back to what the so-called normal person does. He or she shares a small truth slowly over time. These people are smart enough to watch the new friend to see what he or she does with what little information has been conveyed. Emotions (seen in that person's reactions and actions toward you) are very telling and absolutely compelling for why you do or do not share more. As you heal, you learn to be more selective in who you choose as true confidants. To get it right takes a long time while you explore the outer perimeters of trust and trusting.

To heal and advance your struggle to become the best person you can be actually means you will have to eventually reach out with a little bit of your feelings. Pay attention to what transpires. It will speak its truth—trustworthy or not. If you were off target, surgically cut your losses. Walk away—these people are not redeemable. When you need a friend, they do not show up, promises are broken, and these people are walking time bombs when the information you shared is now in the hands of enemy number one. There will be a point where the critical mass blows up in your face. It is not a pretty sight. Reaching out again will be all the harder for the violated.

In my neighbor Peter, I finally found a true friend. I was not seeking a friend when I met him. Why? There was too damn much baggage on my end. I do not respond to pity; I do not want a man to work out my problems. Men, by nature, like to solve a woman's problems. I am certainly no one's problem but my own. Nobody can fix me, since I am not broken. The rest is an inside job. Peter loves me for who I am. He gets that I came by who I am the hard way, but that I am a good person. Very rarely do I share my deepest, darkest feelings with anyone.

Slowly and over time, we became friends. He is a very good man: a heart that sings the same song as mine. My friend is a well-known singer and songwriter, an icon of American folk music. He writes and sings songs about life's struggles; the lyrics of the songs coupled with an amazing ability to stroke his guitar are no different than making mad passionate love. Peter's voice resonates with every phrase, its depth and breath. Most often, the intensity of his feelings are in harmony with mine. We fought different battles. Nonetheless, we understand each other as intimately as any lovers do. I get that he has suffered much through the war, loss of loved ones, and dreams that went south by no fault of his own. I feel his pain as deeply as I feel mine. There is a kinship to which few words are needed; at times, no words need be exchanged. I do not know how we know each other to the extent that we do; we just do. I weep for him as often as I weep for myself. I am blessed to have found a true friend.

Out of his suffering come the richest of songs. His honesty is painfully real in songs about love gone wrong, a nation at war that wants only love, and the beaten and broken people of life. In mastering his craft he is fearless. I have witnessed the process of his songwriting, and it runs in the same vein as he moves through his own emotions. It leaves me in awe. He is mesmerizing to watch: this confluence of talent all jumbled up in one man's heart; his voice and hands are truly the windows to his soul. The brain and heart may function separately, but when they are in sync, there is a great transcendence. I have witnessed this with my own eyes.

He is definitely a man—a love of a lifetime, even if our bodies never connect the way lovers do. I yearn for his whiskey voice that promises me he understands life. He is more real to me than anyone I know. He too struggled to be a true, authentic, and genuine human being. He is noble. The scars of Vietnam are not visible to the naked and undiscerning eye. Only the wounded, those initiated by the passage of life, can look into his eyes to see the pain life has so carelessly dished out—without a thought to the debris it would leave behind. Is life as random as I want to believe? It is a certainty that Peter never did anything to deserve the depth and breadth of the pain he is called upon to bear. I have entrusted him with some of my deepest feelings. I know that those secrets will remain forever safe. I am saddened when he sees me in pain and bears my pain in kind.

Did he really have to know any of it to know me? With all he suffered already, why did I inflict him with my feelings? He could have lived a lifetime without ever knowing my soul. My life would not be as enriched today without trusting him and being trusted in return. For someone so tainted, scared, and stained by life there comes a moment in time when sharing your feelings with someone special feels so right. Why did I choose Peter? What part of him did I see that convinced me that he would take my secrets to the grave? Truthfully, I do not know. I am certain he would never betray me. As my friend, I owe him so much: an apology and a grateful heart—in the end, none of that seems enough. Stay tuned—I think I am falling in love with this man; he just does not know it yet!

Reveling

To revel is to celebrate. It is an exhilaration of life's highest high: a ride to the center of the universe. Stop and smell the roses to celebrate yourself for victories hard-earned. Winning is exhilarating and intoxicating, so much more so than the high of any drug. Why would one want to feel less than they are entitled to feel—a natural high invigorated by life itself? Celebrating victories along the way allows a certain respite from the pain of analysis and the continuing force to push forward.

I, for one, want to stop and celebrate that I have chosen to take the road less traveled. To live a life of mediocrity is not difficult; it is why that is the road most traveled. True joy is not possible on this road, for there is nothing there to be joyous about. To walk the road less traveled is to walk a road where joy abounds, and it requires all the wisdom and wit you have accumulated. Change is scary, and therefore, it is not the choice for the weak or risk-averse. The road less traveled—the one where you become your highest self—is the road you have chosen to follow. Had you made the easier choices in life, you would never have traveled this far. Mediocrity is for the weak—for those who do not want to change their lives for the better. What makes these two types of people so different? Everything: right down to their rose-colored glasses and their half-full glass. Those that travel the road less traveled actually want to participate in making themselves better, and in turn, they make the world around them better.

Yes, I do fault those who select mediocrity. They are the silent souls who never stand up for what is right but let the opportunity go right by them—again and again. The silence of the lambs. Their muscles atrophy—right along with their brain and conscience. Dante reminds us that the ninth circle of Hell is reserved for those who in time of opportunity do not rise to the occasion when the opportunity to do something brave and courageous presents itself. The person who has worked hard to better themselves and the world around them is the person who without thought to consequences does the right thing at the right time for the right reason. These individuals are the everyday heroes in our society. This is why we celebrate what our journeys have brought forth to date. It is almost purifying in some ways because the path has become clearer. You will find that you need a break so that you can start again—renewed with hope, with new strength, and with enlightenment.

Remember to check your calendar on occasion and celebrate your accomplishments. May this process bring you to all of the blessings and abundance that this type of augmentation deserves. Let yourself be celebrated for who you have become, for all your hard work, and for the past pain and fear of struggling. I, too, celebrate you!

THE BED

> "The bed is a place of mystery. It shares our secrets and knows our truths. It is here that we are born. As our lives unfold and we grow older, our relationship with the bed deepens and evolves. Thresholds of experience are crossed here...."
>
> —Unknown

The bed was where I waged my wars, this was my battleground. Many thresholds of experience were crossed here. As a child I was poisoned by unspeakable abuse. I was alone without support. As a young woman, I was driven to succeed in spite of what was done to me. Outwardly, I donned the armor of achievement and success rising to a position of power and influence. I made a conscious choice to build a life that would make anyone proud. Underneath my polished and professional exterior I was always haunted and aware that my past pursued me. I found myself drawn to shattered men, childishly selfish men, and men who hate women even as they tried to love them.

I continually found myself in negative relationships, dangerously so, time after time without understanding why. After years of crossing these thresholds I sought and gained an understanding of myself. But not without great difficulty and pain.

Humankind is complex and complicated. None of us at any one time is just one thing. Much like a diamond, we are multifaceted. If we experience mixed feelings about an area in our lives, our minds are unconsciously pushed for resolution. Conflicts are worked out in our everyday actions. Sometimes, these actions appear diametrically opposed to other areas of our personalities: the librarian who is a hellcat in the bedroom or the professional woman who is promiscuous but a consummate professional in her work arena. To an uninvolved observer, the appearance of such is puzzling.

A normal woman, for whom there is no benchmark, comes into her sexuality in her search for womanhood: a process that is secret, complex, and often delayed by detours. There is no societal rite of passage or social etiquette. How much more complicated it is for the sexually abused woman whose childhood was one of violence, betrayal, and torture. Oftentimes, the sexually abused woman is devoid of feelings: both physically and emotionally. Physically, she equates pain with pleasure. Moreover, more stimulation is necessary based on being highly stimulated at such an early age. These facts require an intimate discussion with a partner. She will stay away from any sexual discussions since the operative word is intimacy. A sexually abused woman is fearful of intimacy because she has been betrayed by the very people entrusted with her early care. She feels that emotions are sticky; feelings are best left for others to experience. Abandonment and rejection are two emotions she will do anything to avoid. If she interacts with men and allows feelings to surface, she must deal with issues of abandonment and rejection. She is incapable of doing so. Thus, the sexually abused woman is a participant in an activity that is fraught with overwhelming challenges.

The Bed

Some women decide to opt out of any sexual interactions. For those women who decide to have a sexual facet to their lives, they do so through the most convoluted and contorted of means. Regardless of how liberated our twenty-first century proclaims to be, society still fears and distorts a woman's sexuality and her unleashed passion.

The word *promiscuity* is often used to define the behavior of an abused woman. Promiscuity is defined as a behavior characterized by casual and indiscriminate sexual intercourse—often with many people. The formal definition leaves us cold; however, the word itself is often associated with women only and carries with it negative inferences. This is especially true in a society that believes men can participate in certain types of behavior that are acceptable because "boys will be boys" but that has a different standard for a woman. For a woman, it is referred to as promiscuity: a word generally used to describe a sexual female trait only.

Many factors influence this search and change over time. The sexually abused woman's search for womanhood is fraught with terror. Whatever means she chooses, it is usually traumatizing, and future interactions become daunting. Sexual healing is brought about when the survivor connects his or her current sexual behavior to past sexual abuses.

REVENGE FOR THE SINS OF MY FATHER

Today, my past sexual exploitations are embarrassing. As a young woman, there was a dark side that I passionately explored. Unconsciously, I drove myself through acts of pain and depravation: my exterior tough; my interior hardwiring, a disaster. Devoid of feelings, my territorial boundaries were uncharted. Told throughout my life I was nothing, I was inevitably going to be something—and a sexually dangerous woman at that.

If my bed could speak, it would relay some of the most hair-raising adventures—jungle sex at its best and the most unspeakable acts of eroticism—all that transpires behind closed doors. In my own defense, I am forced to seek out electrical tape to ensure the silence of my bed. I turn shades of red when I flash back to some of the things I have done to pleasure men. The bed was where I waged my wars. I sought revenge, ensured my own punishment, and discovered my womanhood while holding the only trump card I later discovered was mine: addicting these men into a sexually erotic relationship. God help those sinners that thought I was ever so compliant to their desires. I more than met their needs. Men feel that women are replaceable: one easily substituted for another. About needs, men are clueless. Ruthlessly exploiting these men, I brought a whole new meaning to the word *need*. Soon, they craved the very thing I had to offer. Men, I learned, are genetically predisposed to sexual perversions—no different from an addict genetically predisposed to drug addictions. This reality is as basic to a man's everyday ability to survive as the air he breathes and the water he consumes to hydrate. I was wicked, shameless, and deadly. God help them. They never had a prayer.

Initially, I was not conscious of what I was doing—until years later. Sex was a compelling force within me that overrode any other thoughts. I had a seriously deranged mind. In the beginning, my behavior felt perfectly normal. Pain begets pain; it seeks its own level.

Having engaged in a heated telephone conversation with the man I had slept with the night before, I felt nothing but fury. My anger was most likely directed toward myself and projected onto him for the slightest transgression. I hung the phone up and distanced myself from any possible interruptions. I sat on the commode—head in my hands—and wept. I remember staring at my crumpled bed. Out of my lips emerged a blood-curdling cry: a deep primal scream so hair-raising that my neighbors called 911. It was not until some moments later that I realized the deep resonating cries were coming from within the vortex of my soul. The wounded woman within me rose up and angrily ripped the bed apart. My rage toward the bed was real—accusing me of every whorish act conceivable to humankind. I stripped the bed of its trappings; furiously, I ripped at the sheets and the blankets, tearing them off and yelling, "Is this it? Is this all there is to my life?" In the middle of this storm, I was able to soothe neither the child within me nor the wounded woman I had become.

The bed was my undoing. It was no secret that my life as I knew it began there. The real question was whether my life would end there as well. My questions seemed fundamentally simple; the answers, not so much. The question, when objectively stated, was whether Mary Elizabeth was destined to be defined by these experiences. At some point, I sentenced myself: *Guilt deserves punishment.* I programmed the men in my life to punish me. I set them up to leave me. There was such a profound need in me to suffer: to feel searing pain, to loathe the very idea of me, and ultimately designed to ensure I received all the pain I righteously deserved.

I profoundly understood the pain of rejection and loss—the very two emotions I feared the most. *I anticipate you will abandon me, and I will grieve when the inevitable arrives.* In retrospect, my attachments to men were difficult. My secrets were always well guarded; there were no chinks in my armor. I expected betrayal—a self-fulfilling prophecy. A sexually abused woman never gives all of her heart to one man but to a parade of men—always someone waiting in the wings. I learned early on to diversify my risks. The ability to surgically cut your losses is that much cleaner and, by definition, controls the pain.

After the loss of each man, I became more callous. I thought to myself: *Go and be yourself—just be yourself somewhere else and not around me.* I never looked back—not once. Spoken aloud, I said, "Next," and I meant it with precious few tears to shed.

All of this pain led me to conclude that I purposely did this to myself. I was hell-bent on self-destruction. I came to realize during some of my darkest moments that there was no one to blame but myself, and no one on the visible horizon appeared remotely capable of stopping me in this deadly process. In that stark moment, I realized no earthly power could save my soul from spiraling down the path of self-destruction. I had no doubt I would die this way. Mr. Goodbar was going to win. My predisposition for tall, dark, and dangerously handsome men never abated. This was my addiction, and it would be the death of me. My attitude and engrained behavior left me in a no-win situation.

Judging Me

When agitated by the man in my life, I gave the usual annoyance glance, and it was over. There was even a point where I no longer cared to give that steamy look of an "I-will-kill-you" glare. No, I was in it for penny and for pound. The best revenge for me was to let men bleed out slowly. My goal was to addict them, use them, and then end it with the type of look that starkly manifested my disgust: "If I could, I would penetrate your skin and perforate a vital organ or two." I was not someone to be messed with. This was a dangerous and deadly dance. Somebody was going to get hurt, and that somebody was me.

My Sexual Philosphy
I Know Men and I Know Them Well

I know a sinner when I see one. Game on. I was not some sweet little thing you would take home to mother; rather, I was just the opposite. Because I was often perceived as a "Barbie" doll, men had no idea of who I was or the pain I was capable of inflicting. I was not anyone's "Barbie" doll.

I am a complicated package—with a thousand-megahertz mind—and fearlessly independent. I am a woman of a certain age. I am a woman of power with the determination and the intensity of an atomic blast. As a woman, I am sexual and sensual.

Oh, The Sweet Possibilities

A woman who has come into her own is a formidable and fearsome creature—a woman of substance, with a past. She is a world-class whore in the bedroom, a lady in the living room, and a leader in the boardroom. Beware. She is capable of mentally eviscerating a man in less than ten seconds. She will probe the depths of your psyche to challenge your balance. She will bring you to your proverbial knees with ecstasy, decimating any boundaries of fantasies to the sweet possibilities. She will own you. Make no mistake: if you are not man enough to embrace the probabilities, she can and will destroy you. Her power is exhilarating but devastating. Only a fool would engage such a woman without fully considering the consequences.

A megahertz mind commands loyalty. She will tempt you and pleasure you. She crosses boundaries that will weaken you and demand her full worth from your soul. If you betray her because you are weak, she will be ruthless. She possesses a love that can launch ten thousand ships and a passion that will singe your soul. Cross her, and she will scorch the earth, burying your ashes.

Do you know this woman? For it was I....
Existential Epiphanies

The sex was always hot and explosive as I drove through a man's primordial forces with such sweet pain that an otherwise conscious body could not endure. It was my animal directness and the perversity of my needs that shattered their cerebral restraint. My ruthless directness in seeking to satisfy my own needs kept them in a state of constant arousal. Aware, they went through their days with a woman who commanded respect from her peers and who was loved by her family and admired by her friends—all the while knowing that her true nature was such that no one in their insular world could have believed or imagined it. They reveled in my unrestrained eroticism. I gave the orders, and they obeyed them. Men abased themselves before me, worshipping at the pagan altar of my sex. I always demanded an answer to what had to be a wet dream: "What am I to you, Big Boy? Say it! I am your whore!"

Only after my deepest desires were sated to some degree could I focus on kissing, exploring, and caressing men. I was usually ready for them before we were alone; I could not get my clothes off fast enough. Sometimes, I didn't bother to remove them; other times, I wore skirts so short that I could simply astride them in the car or lift my leg in a fortuitous hallway, elevator, or bathroom, where I could take them standing up. I fucking dared them to take me in crowded places, where discovery would have instantly shattered the perfect image granted to us by our professions. The riskier the possibilities of discovery, the more I taunted. It is only now that I realize that the game as it was played really hurt no one but me. Men, once they kicked their habit—although few today have—only cared about one thing: sex. Perhaps, had I been wiser and older, I would have demanded material possessions for my time. There was no doubt that I earned whatever diamond or fur I collected. Yet, there was not one single thing a man could offer me that I could not provide for myself—on any level. Asking for anything made me feel weak and vulnerable.

After a time, I grew weary of training men in the sport of bedroom etiquette. It was not the act of fucking but my own deranged mentality. There are many ways to achieve orgasm. The missionary position: do not like it; do not do it. The acts then escalate to erotica. Erotica includes a variety of sexual acts that most men enjoy with their girlfriends. Girlfriends are willing participants for some of these fantasies—but not all. At the far end of erotica—which were the illegal and deadly acts—was not a place I wanted to go. Back up to those acts prior to there, and you have every man's delicious fantasy. This is the place where the probability of addiction arises: a dangerous point for those who are not aware of what lies in wait—minefields built on thermite bombs. The temperature is off the rector scale. What man would not come back for more?

It came to the point where there was nothing in it for me anymore. My part was always about pleasuring men. What they failed to realize is that a woman with my sexual background can rarely be satisfied. Men are so into their own pleasure that, after a while, they seek precious little else. Once a pattern such as this began to develop, I knew it was only a matter of time before I ended the aforementioned theatrics. Propped up against the door, looking as sexy as one can after six or eight hours of mind-blowing sex, eyes steamed over, I said when he was most vulnerable: "You were simply a mind fuck to me—nothing more; nothing less. You bore me. Now get out!" Nothing ended it like this.

The absolute truth: I was bored; I did not want or like this game anymore. I never liked games of any kind. Initially, it never occurred to me that this was a conscious game. Only later did I grasp the concept that, in seeking revenge, I developed a pattern and practice to my behavior that amounted to a game of sorts. It was then that I came to realize that I would have killed for a real man who had the insight to call me on my own issues. The men I selected were some of the most brilliant men in the universe but without an ounce of common sense: giants in their respective fields, weak as hell in the bedroom, and without a clue as to what to do with me.

Except one. He cracked through my defense mechanisms, and the walls started to crumble. This was clearly unacceptable for me. Absolutely fucking brilliant, baby blues...but nothing, or so I thought, between the color of his eyes and his professional work. I thought this would work out fine for me as I was no more interested in a relationship than flying to the moon. With velvet gloves, he called me on my stuff. "Nicely done," I thought. I actually liked his perceptiveness, and I began to enjoy his companionship. He moved in on my heart like no one else. I was in trouble, and I had the sense to know it. He taught me more about myself than anyone. He knew what and how to push my triggers; that pissed the hell out of me. The first time he did this, he asked, "Don't you think the punishment you doled out to me is far worse than the alleged crime you accuse me of? Do I have to take it for all the other assholes in your life? And remember: *you* picked them." I had a righteous mad going, and as much as I wanted to keep it that way, I found I could not. He was right on the money. He blew me away—silence. It sounds vapid in retrospect; I too was not dumb by any means—just blindsided. The very first time he called me on my issues, I began to feel more passion for him than I had ever experienced. My own issues were surfacing so quickly while I had escalated his. Between the two of us, he scared me, while having nothing to fear from me. I did not appreciate that he saw so much good in me and knew me for what and who I really was: a kitten in need of a kindhearted master. And it was not so much about the sex as it was about the heart. To this day, I cannot run my sex games with him. The truth is: I cannot go there even if I want to. I still do not quite grasp or understand the dynamics at work. Maybe I never will. I pretend as if I do not care when I desperately do. Perhaps I am afraid of actually falling in love; this makes me raw and easy prey. God help me, he could be the death of me by kindness. Who would figure I might die at the hands of a kind man who understood my own complexities? I thought: *Oh hell to the no.* If I repeat this often enough, I might really mean it—not. I think I am actually confused, as I really know men; I just do not get me— no doubt, a precarious position for someone in my shoes.

There was dramatic tension in the bedroom that played itself out. I used sex as a means of power and control. It was my way of capturing the man, regardless of whether I sought submission or pain. I pushed myself onward to lose control—to find that place beyond rational consciousness—as a means of transcendence and even as escape. The two sides were always in tension, and even I did not always know which side would emerge the stronger.

At times, I have a sense of both sides of me simultaneously: vulnerable and venerated at the same time is a compelling representation of who I really am. In part, it is my way of proving that I am a survivor. The delightful complexities of human nature never cease to fascinate all participants. Whether I decide to be in control from the top down or the bottom up is anyone's guess. It is always about control: theirs and mine, eluding the possession of the undeniably complicated woman that I have become.

I never wanted to belong to anyone, except him. Sex with him was not so much about capturing him as it was about being captured.

Men – A Broken Creep Meter

I wonder if there are some relationships in life that stay with you forever: that as an adult, you never recover from or forget. I am not referring to parental or sibling relationships but to relationships of the heart that sear your soul in such a way that you are never the same person—not just in the moment but in every moment thereafter. There are experiences that go beyond words. Thoughts of that person continue to flow throughout your life. I believe there are such past relationships that profoundly affect you in the present and for all time. This is why I briefly share with you three of the deepest and most memorable relationships I experienced that still haunt my soul today.

They say men come into our lives for a reason, a season, or a lifetime. For me it was a reason—a lesson to be learned. After each blow, I convinced myself that in a few months' time, I would be over him: a scarce memory. Only, that was never true. These experiences exist in my conscious memory to this very day, frightening me for fear of ever going back to that type of man again. There is a reason. I know it, and you know it. I could wax poetically about how I fell in love with each man, but it would be such hypocrisy at this point, that to do so now would seem foolish.

Love is a very special feeling for me. Men generally, on the other hand, are able to pretend that matters of the heart do not matter: freezing out the one they love. Always, my heart is in danger; the directive is to rid myself of the spiritual blockages that constrict my emotions, creativity, or analytical thought processes and which bring forth feelings of anger, fear, and resentment. Love cannot flow freely at this juncture. My heart hurts when it is not at peace. I cannot invest my time, creative energy, and emotion in anything else but making the situation right between us. I cannot focus. Plenty is happening around me, impatiently awaiting the attention I do not have. I am struggling to hold on to the center of my universe. Getting to the heart of the matter is the only damn thing that matters: a soul-directed impulse; a sacred imperative. Men and women differ so greatly in matters of the heart; it is a wonder that we communicate at all.

There was never a doubt that in a crowded room, I would select the single most dangerous man, and he too would laser in on me. Damaged people attract damaged people. Although their individual faces were different, their professions were dissimilar, and their style was unique, I knew deep down inside of me they were ultimately going to be my father all over again.

The definition of insanity is doing the same thing over and over again and expecting different results. This is the pattern of an abused woman whether she realizes it or not. Whether she really *wants* different results is a topic for another day. Nevertheless, I did.

My creep meter was in need of a major overhaul. After reading about three of my relationships, you will easily discern that I dislike men as much as the men I selected disliked women. However, the lessons learned were invaluable.

He Whose Name We Dare Not Breathe (Hereafter Referred To As "The Control Freak")

This man taught me some of the most difficult lessons in love to learn. There is always one person in the relationship who loves more than the other does. It is a bitch if the person who loves more just happens to be you. Of course, you will not know this until the end—or pretty near to it.

This man understood women and was all the more dangerous for it. He placed me under a microscope, and like a specimen to a scientist, the plot to undo me began. Anyone that knows me is aware of my barren landscape, where any act of kindness feels like rain on my soul. As a lover, he discounted and devalued me. He tried to destroy me mentally and emotionally, and in giving him my body, he appropriated every aspect of my being. This was control at its most cruel and hard edge. His first strategy, however, was to weaken me: control the natural outgrowth. He messed with my head. He kept me off-center and confused. He told me my anger pushed him away. *Projection*, I thought. After the first year of the relationship, he said, "This is just too heavy for me. Can't we be light and easy?" I told him, "No problem; consider it done."

My thoughts said it all: *Read between the lines, Asshole—adios. Next.*

Once he was sated sexually, he immediately rolled over and managed to go to sleep, unconcerned with my own sexual gratification. I wanted to kick him in the ass. I made sure to inform him that under no circumstances should he ever "leave me wanting."

In other words: not a problem; I will find someone else to meet my needs—closed issue.

Once accustomed to his sexual rejection, I waited for him to fall asleep. Since I had so much pent-up sexual energy, I needed to do something, and work was my drug of choice. I got out of bed with the stealth of an adulterer to slip inside my office down the hall. The law is a jealous mistress. I thought he understood my infidelities. I thought he accepted my need to be alone and work. After all, he fell asleep—what was it to him that I left the bedroom? There was nothing there for me. I never realized how much this hurt him. I thought he was used to my late-night peregrinations when I could not sleep. I worked through the night on any legal motions or briefs that were due—sometimes into the wee hours of the morning. These were my best hours to think and accomplish some of my finest work—the telephone did not ring, and people did not pull me in a zillion directions. I craved the silence of the early morning hours when the rest of the world was still asleep. The absolute aloneness of self—when the rest of the world was unconscious—created a feeling of peace and oneness with the world. Besides, what did he care? His argument of being abandoned in bed fell on deaf ears. I told him to curl up with a soft pillow. I refused to lie beside him and steam about his insensitivities.

Working through the night was actually my normal working hours. They seemed so routine to me—almost mundane—until inspected by others, especially him. This was when I realized that I did not live my life like other people. My talents propelled me into success. I was a mystery to others. Confused, they did not understand me and felt threatened by me. There was a difference between my cognitive abilities and a skill set that was uniquely my own. A woman I hold in the highest esteem said to me one day, "You are undoubtedly the brightest, most creative woman I know." At a later point in time, someone else repeated the very same comment to me. Struck by these remarks, I wondered about the truthfulness. Were people just being nice, or did they really feel that way? I always felt "less than…." In trying to transform myself, these comments helped me to realize much of my unlimited potential. I was very confused by this misunderstanding of myself with others.

The Control Freak intentionally set out to make me feel insecure about my success. After I had won a particularly difficult motion, he asked me if I was really sure I won. Nothing about my talent, skills, or abilities felt admirable to him.

He chastised me for just about everything, making me feel downright sleazy. The very thing that attracted him to me—my short skirts, my stilettos, my eye makeup, my own sense of style that uniquely made me different from other women—was the very thing that drove him away in the end. Trust a man to make you feel insecure right down to your most cherished accessories!

A dialogue is an elegant term to describe what always shaped up to be a real cluster "fuck." Between us, any type of dialogue became a virtual impossibility. After a while, we completely lost the ability to communicate. He was an alcoholic; all he could think about was the bottle. He took his frustrations out on me. Damn the bottle! One day when he came back to my apartment, he called me a *whore*. I looked around my apartment, thinking: *He cannot possibly be talking to me.* I said, "Are you talking to me?" He looked at me, and from that moment on, I knew this relationship was over. When he left, I slowly went into my bedroom and packed up his belongings. When he came back, I handed him his box of personal items and asked for my house key. He was in shock. Mr. Tall, Dark, and Handsome never had a woman kick him out. I relayed the following, "You must find your own salvation to set you free, and that is not me. I am not your mother, sister, or therapist.

I am your lover." He left just as I asked, and it tore me apart. I really did love him. Remember what I said about the one who loves more in a relationship? That was me, and I was righteously devastated. He was my lesson to learn; I was his castle to burn. God, the months that followed were worse than withdrawing from any chemical substance I could imagine.

Just when I thought I was over him, he called to ask me out on a date. Was this a curtain call? The invitation was an opening salvo not a time for closure. I no longer sucked the air out of the room when I heard his voice. I thought aloud, "Is this something I will have to survive all over again? And, if so, I am not up to it." No way was I going back there. It was only a matter of time until he reverted to form. In the time we spent together, I came to understand that he actually hated women. Sexually abused as a small boy by his mother and sister, he could not come to grips with why he did what he did to women. He sought solace in alcohol. As women, we spend so much time trying to figure men out; however, we never get to know the real answer. The word *closure* is nothing but psychobabble for an opening salvo where one party wants to get back together. Why, when I was over my addiction to this man, would I want to reengage, knowing he would revert to his old ways? Sure, I had my own craziness to work through; I just was not *that* crazy.

He Whose Name I Often Wonder
(Hereafter Referred To As "The One That Got Away")

I met him after breaking up with the Control Freak. I had grieved so long for the man I let go of that I was not interested in returning any other man's telephone calls—especially someone

I had met the night before. I must admit that he was persistent. I looked at my call slips and simply trashed them. After a few months, a mutual friend called me and relayed that this gentleman had been unable to contact me. She asked if I would take his call. Reluctantly, I told her that I would be home for another half hour, and if he did not call by then, I would be difficult to reach. He did call me, and he wanted to take me out for coffee and maybe to a bookstore. My girlfriend must have relayed the same. This was personally my idea of a great first date as these were two of my favorite things. I wondered how he knew or if they were his favorite too. I still ached for my last lover, and I was not sure that letting anyone new into my life was healthy for either of us.

He was so convincing and sweet that I capitulated. He seemed so honest and sincere—not to mention the fact that he was still calling me months later after we met: not in a stalker-like fashion, just enough to let me know he was interested. After a few cancellations on my part, I finally ran out of excuses. He was a delightful surprise. I later discovered that he spent the time between asking me out and our first date learning about various coffee houses, coffee drinks, and the different ways of ordering coffee according to where you were. He did not even drink coffee. Best of all, he found a great bookstore that contained a coffeehouse within the store. This touched the soft, tender spots in my heart. No one that I was aware of spent so much time preparing for that first night out just to impress me. He was a special man for sure.

In fairness to him, I disclosed that very evening that I was just coming out of a long-term relationship and was frankly not relationship material. He made an interesting and endearing comment: "The dust has to settle sometime, and I would like to be around when it does." How great was that? Not to mention, I later learned he was absolutely great in bed. I was taken by the attention and true devotion to me. He was the very opposite of the Control Freak.

Following my judicial appointment, he singlehandedly moved me to Los Angeles. He could not do enough for me. So, what did Mary Elizabeth do? You guessed it; I screwed it up. I will take full responsibility for the disaster that ensued. His actions thereafter were manipulative and cruel. Did I not ask for that, after all?

Once he made up his mind that my crime was unforgiveable, my tried and true defense mechanisms assessed he had a limited mind—at that. He, however, decided to play me. He was a real ass, but had I not asked for it? At that point, we had absolutely nothing in common but extraordinary sex. Passion was the great equalizer for us. We never could bring each other anything but a world of trouble. Since pain was all I knew, we stayed together for years—on and off. It was about the sex; it was always about the sex. He became a very difficult person after a while. I found I no longer knew this man, and ultimately, he hurt me more often than he brought me joy. He was punishing me for breaking his heart and has been doing so for years. I could not blame him in the least. Although, at some point, you would figure I had paid the price.

As time passed and I had declared war on accepting anyone in my life that was not life-enhancing, it was time to surgically cut him loose. It was always about whether someone or something was life-diminishing or life-enhancing. I had to end all ties with him—which was especially difficult since the sex was so explosive. I never forgot that I had someone very special until I screwed it up. Hearts are so very fragile, especially the heart of a man. Women are more used to forgiving; not men, as they bury themselves in their man cave to lick their wounds. Men have learned that the deep pain I dished out was uniquely from the type of a woman referred to through the centuries as a "siren song."

Later, I learned that he too had a reason to dislike women. He had never respected his mother because of her infidelities to his father. He had no reason to trust me or any woman and every reason not to trust me in particular. I will always wonder what would have happened if I had not screwed things up from the beginning. Could he have been Mr. Right? That is something I will never know.

He Whose Name We Do Not Speak
(Hereafter Referred To As "The Pig")

This was the very last and worst of my adventures into the type of love I so frequently sought, and love him I did. He knew me as no other man had—like no other man ever will. Until then, I never understood what it meant to be steeped in someone. Until then, I had not wanted to. This was the first and only time I let my mind go and experienced lovemaking as it was meant to be: a mindless and liberating pleasure. In surrendering my mind, my best defense was completely disabled.

I originally assumed that, as a member of law enforcement, he had integrity. That was their slogan after all. I was never so wrong. He learned that I was a federal civil rights judge, and he had a federal civil rights case. This is why all of a sudden he was very interested in me. I should have known it was about what he could get from me and not about me. He saw me as useful and nothing else. He was a superb liar and a great manipulator. I spent nearly three years with this man before I saw him as he really was. Do not get me wrong: I saw plenty of warning signals, but I was in the middle of my own personal crisis. I can only deal with one major crisis at a time. His usefulness for me had not ended, however. Why he could not have asked me as a friend to listen to him rather than rope me in as his lover was anybody's guess. It was his hatred for his mother and all women. He idealized his father (who either maimed or killed his mother during a domestic violence dispute). The philosophy was to manipulate her, beat her up, and then kill the bitch.

This man was a liar and a thief. He brought me only pain. Being in the highest form of law enforcement he had every resource available to him to check out his mother's death. Oddly, he never did. Instead, he idolized his father, who rejected him and forced him to live with his uncle. He said he loved me, and I wanted to believe it. I was the biggest fool. He did what he could to destroy me: he stole from me; he lied about leaving his wife; he lived in two places at once while he told me he pulled a second shift; and he began a relationship with my assistant—all to make a mockery of me and everything I stood for.

When it was finally over, I was never more relieved. The only retribution I had was inadvertent. At his trial, I could not testify as his character witness or for his pain and suffering. Actually, I ended up testifying for the other side. I never planned it this way. The fact that he literally only wanted to use me—lied, manipulated, played me, and began an affair with my assistant while being engaged to marry me—created in me an enormous mistrust – an understatement at best. In the end, this made it impossible for me to testify that he was a man well deserving of his promotion, and that the emotional injuries he suffered were real, based on his employer's failure to legitimately promote him. I could not testify to something I no longer held to be true or when I had reasons to suspect that everything he conveyed to me was a lie. He was untruthful to me on every level.

This man gave a whole new definition to the term *unavailable*. He had a way of making me so mad that I envisioned setting his hair on fire. I have never hated someone before, but he instilled in me the worst feelings I had for any human being. In my life, I disliked many people intensely, but I never hated them. To hate another person is wrong. Hatred is a crime of the spirit that leads to crimes of the flesh. Used and abused are not my favorite emotions, and he came as close as any man in replicating my father in every aspect. I have never felt this way about anyone else, and I do not think I ever will.

In summary, the theme in each of these relationships is the same: men who do not like women and women who dislike men. Until these men revealed their past to me, I did not have a clue as to how they felt about women, even when I initially questioned them about their family life. Had I known, I would have run like hell. I was already aware that I should never be around a man that hates his mother or blames her for some gross transgressions which may or may not be true. It really does not matter whether she was guilty as charged; it is only about their perception of the truth. No woman deserves to be murdered. What kind of man could rationalize his mother's death at the hands of his father and consider it okay? This man could have been my Mr. Goodbar. I thank God that my senses were hyper-vigilant. There was an internal warning that told me I was unsafe around him. After that I never wanted to be alone with him. My dog nipped him on the way out the door. I patted her on the head and gave her a dividend for having such discerning taste. This relationship ended very poorly.

I have always believed and acted on the belief that relationships should end elegantly. Who needs the knock-down, drag-out kind of ending or the scorched-earth policy? Who and what does it serve to destroy each other at the very end? When you know a relationship is over and that it is unredeemable, why not end it as elegantly as possible? However, it takes two people to rise above any petty self-vindictiveness that could easily transpire. Only you can decide how you will act or react. What another person does is on him or her. You cannot decide for others how to act. Once a Pig, always a Pig. Walk away from a relationship with as much self-integrity as you can. The world is a very small place; as a result, you never know whose path you will cross again and in what way.

THERAPY

With childhood sexual abuse like mine, some type of long-term intense therapy was inevitable. My new therapist was both a spiritual counselor and a psychologist.

Initially, I started therapy in my early twenties, thinking a few sessions would cure my free-floating anxiety attacks. I was driving to work one day when I felt as if I were having a heart attack. I pulled off to the side of the road, and a highway patrolman called an ambulance. You can imagine my embarrassment when the doctor told me I had a panic attack—not a heart attack—and that next time, I should breathe into a paper bag. My doctor asked me a few probing questions about the general status of my life. I relayed to him that I was Catholic and happily married with two small children. I do not know what compelled me to answer in that manner. In any event, the doctor recommended therapy. I took his advice, and seven years later, I wondered why my happy ass was still sitting in the same chair. Obviously, I was not so happy and had so many issues I wondered if I would be in this same chair another seven years. The very thought petrified me, so I decided to take a break. During this seven-year period, I had gone through a divorce, been remarried, and changed careers. My life had drastically changed. No wonder the emergency room doctor recommended therapy. I am not a good liar; like Pinocchio, my nose grows.

My second experience with therapy was when my fight-or-flight button was stuck; the problem was to figure out how to get unstuck in the moment which seemed to be hovering near perpetuity. These were scary times; I was finally unstuck, so I viewed therapy as successful. In retrospect, I should have stayed in therapy as my life was spiraling down into a black hole. I did not stay and instead took another long break. Perhaps, had I stayed in therapy, my behavior would not have skyrocketed out of control. I needed to hit bottom before my therapist's insights would have any meaning to me.

Ultimately, my behavior with men got me into real trouble. My personal life was a disaster—although my professional life was at its best. I had a firm rule that I relayed to the men in my life: if anyone caused me grief that spilled over into my career, that effected or interfered with my professional life, the relationship was *over*. A thick and impenetrable wall compartmentalized my relationship with men and my work. I loved my work; it defined me. Work was my drug of choice. If I needed to get out of my head, I worked. If I was in crisis mode, I worked. The precision of my work as an attorney soothed me until I could mentally work out my other issues. When my sexual antics got in the way of my work, I immediately headed back for therapy, but this time it felt different.

Enlightenment came none too soon. My therapist asked me, "Have you ever considered that your life reads like one of your complicated cases: due to this or that, and on and on?" It was my karma to return to the original scene of the crime: the original loss of my father. Irma (my therapist) relayed, "You are a student of the violated, always hoping to undo what can never be changed. You repeat the behavior—the oldest pattern in human nature. It is not one damn thing after another; rather, it is the same thing over and over again." She went on to explain that, as a child, I shut down. This, she explained, led to denial. When you deny the past, you are doomed to repeat it. That was not something I was eager to hear; yet, I knew she spoke the truth. Tragically, she summed it up by stating, "Your life has been one loss after another after the original crime of your father." Ironically, she stated, "You have turned loss into a profession; a pattern like this, if not arrested, takes on an unstoppable energy, where you will be sucked into a black vortex from which you may never return." I did not want to hear this, and I did not want to believe what she stated. I knew she spoke the truth. I did not want to go through that looking glass one more time.

I sincerely believed that if I choose not to acknowledge the sexual involuntary images and associations that ran through my mind, I could avoid the unbearable suffering that I would most certainly invite. Therapy was hard work. Now, all that mattered was getting better. Ultimately, the men and the games I played were more than I could handle; it brought me to my knees. I realized this entire mess brought me no gifts but stole from my soul, further torturing me and scarring my psyche.

I was so anxious to get well and transform my life that therapy seemed to move faster—even though my issues were more complicated. I wound up going back through the looking glass to my father and the initial betrayals. Irma saw my present life as a direct result of the past. She took no prisoners and spoke the truth, even when it was painful to hear. I knew I was making progress; my life was indeed transforming, and my spirituality was moving through the core of who I was. Irma was a treasure: a woman I respected as I grew to see my reality through her eyes. She bestowed the power upon me to overcome most of my obstacles, always inspiring in me the drive to push through the pain.

> "It is not the tragedies that kill us—
> but the messes!"
>
> —Dorothy Parker

*To Saint Jude, Patron Saint of lost causes,
and attorneys who are always in over their heads*

WHY LAW SCHOOL?

Indeed, this was a very good question. I disliked attorneys as much as anyone else did. Lawyer jokes were, to me, righteously earned. The rationale for the completion of my MBA was to be an effective and efficient businessperson. Two things happened that pushed me into entering law school: The first was my position as an elected official for a pilot program stemming from the Public Utilities Commission (PUC), referred to as Utilities Consumer Action Network (UCAN). The second event that propelled me into law school was a mayoral appointment to the Election, Campaign, and Governmental Ethics Advisory Board.

Why would anyone in their right mind—with an already full plate—sign up for a position as a board member for a PUC pilot project that paid no money? First, the summer prior to the election, I received a gas and electric bill of $750, while my family and I were out of town. When I called to inquire about the mistake in the charges, the customer service representative relayed the following: "We do not make mistakes." I was shocked. Entities consist of human beings. They make mistakes, even with advanced technology. Machines make mistakes. I said, "Let me speak to your supervisor." She, too, relayed the same party line. Angry (and now edgy, with a flinty tone to my voice), I inquired, "What would happen if I could not pay this bill?" With a tart and smartass attitude, she stated, "Your power would be shut off immediately." Beyond enraged, I hung the up the telephone. Later, my husband ponied up the money.

Still fuming about the very arrogance of such a monopoly, I spotted an announcement in our daily newspaper: a one-inch-by-one-inch column that stated that the PUC was seeking to elect individuals to preside as a watchdog agency for our gas and electric. I was invigorated. This was the perfect opportunity to initiate changes against the behemoth that purported perfectionism. The county consumers were certain to benefit from an overdue attitude adjustment. I was sure I was not the only scorned consumer. It would be impossible for any mammoth entity to withstand such strict scrutiny. After having my petition signed off by registered voters, my name went on the ballot. Without any money to actually campaign, I procured the names and telephone numbers of all my east county constituents. Then, I broke my back in a traffic accident. I was laid up in the hospital for weeks, which made campaigning very difficult. Instead of sending out flyers, I called almost every consumer in my district. I beat a current politician by eleven votes—a close race indeed.

My first real physical act was a joint audit of the nuclear power plants. I discovered gross cost overruns, price gouging, fraud, and other violations of the law as enumerated by PUC regulations. Most county residents received a rebate of two hundred to nine hundred dollars. Doing the math was easy; however, overseeing such a large monopoly and drafting firm and clear legislation was another reality—one usually reserved for attorneys.

The second critical set of circumstances arose when I became a mayoral appointee to the Election, Campaign, and Governmental Ethics Advisory Board. The board held public hearings with various facets of government. These hearings were a forum that examined some of the weakest links in each of the entities. Discussions, suggestions, and expert testimony helped to determine the needed changes, while allowing the public to air their grievances. Again, I realized that one needed a law degree to make firm, clear, legislative mandates without loopholes.

Granted, my contributions were significant: intellectual, arrived at through deductive reasoning, and accompanied with the appropriate rationale for much-needed changes. My ideas led to logical conclusions; however, they never seemed to be more than a suggestion at best. Law school seemed inevitable. I felt that my contributions would have been greater had I been able to follow through with written legislative mandates.

LAW SCHOOL

At first blush, the weak and lazy walk away from the daunting law school admission process. The rest of us question our sanity when we ask ourselves, "Oh, God, do I really want to do this?" My way of addressing the overwhelming and numerous tasks required for admission was to chunk down each step in the process. This was the only way to address all of the prior requisites. Managing the tasks made completing them more palatable.

The next step is preparation for the Law School Admission Test (LSAT), which, like the MCAT, does not determine what kind of student you will be or how successful a lawyer or doctor you will become. Law schools admit the truth of the matter, but they feel there must be some way to guesstimate which students will survive law school, graduate, and go on to practice law. The preparation for the LSAT is a matter of deciding that you will be the best LSAT-taker in your preparation class. This requires a dedicated, completely focused, and disciplined student who understands the need for tunnel vision. The prelaw student must be willing to sacrifice his or her summer or a semester of social events. It is during this time the student must take all of the prior LSAT exams repeatedly—until he or she scores in the ninetyish percentile. Over-preparation never hurts anyone. Under-preparation actually does since it erodes an applicant's self-confidence.

Judging Me

The word *judgment* is no longer spelled with the letter *e*, and you no longer *think* or *feel*; rather, *the court holds*. These are the first two things a law student learns in the first days of class.

I was older than most of my peers. Typically, law school students enter right after college graduation. Students fresh out of college have a party mentality. Study time was sporadic and quality time in shorter supply. Ah, to be young and still be willing to beat yourself up in an already tortuous process.

Instantly instilled in the first-year law student is sheer fear—especially if no one prepared you in advance that your homework assignments were pre-assigned over the summer. Thus, numbers of first-year students who walk into class the first day are set up for the most unpleasant of surprises: humiliation, embarrassment, and mortification. Your classmates will laugh, and your professors will not forget that you were unprepared. Classmates, as a rule, do not share or work well together. Law school is just as adversarial as the practice of law. This is why we later refer to each other as opposing counsel.

Law school as depicted in the 1973 film, *The Paper Chase*, perfectly describes this moronic behavior. Hiding books, old practice exams, misinformation, and sheer intimidation work well on fellow students—unlike medical school, where the institution as a whole works to ensure all who entered those halls will, with or without help, receive their medical degree. Law school is another story: it weeds out what students they believe to be weak without a second thought as to whether they could pass and become excellent attorneys. The weeding-out process is continuous through graduation. Prior to my first exam, I stopped off at the restroom, only to find all the stalls filled with vomiting classmates. This sent chills up my spine as it would any first year student. Law school students, your peers, get off on the hype they make regarding the difficulty of the assignments or exams. (I avoided this type of craziness at all costs. There was nothing like an afternoon of retail therapy to set a girl's mind straight.)

In an effort to graduate from law school, the student also had to rely on law professors. Reliance on their help was an oxymoron. It was simply abominable to experience the unreachable, untouchable, and always unavailable professors. The students then rely on one another, which was a formula for disaster. Pranks and the failure of certain members of your study group to keep their promises to outline certain chapters were predictable. The goal was to keep your cool and never let anyone see you sweat.

Law school is a microcosm of the bigger world of legal practitioners. It is the rite of initiation and the key to the passage of all doors. Law school is your introduction into the world of first-class cheats, affirming the notion that hiding the ball will ensure their success while destroying others. Very few students thrive during law school; most are lucky to survive. No one, and I mean no one, cares whether you manage to succeed or fail. The professors make it known that there are far too many lawyers already: therein is the administrative justification for quickly weeding out students. I, for one, thought the process itself was inhumane. I could only imagine how much worse it would get with the practice of law. I was not disappointed in the least.

Law school in no way prepares an attorney to practice law, run an office, and be an ethical or decent human being. If you started law school without knowing the difference between right and wrong, you were sure to excel in the practice of law. Courses on ethics teach students the intricacies of not becoming the target of a state bar investigation while skirting the professional rules of conduct. During the process of inculcating legal maneuvers, it teaches each student how to talk out of both sides of their mouth—a skill set only learned in law school. This particular skill set ensures unethical and immoral behavior. Law school teaches you to disregard your natural gut instinct, set aside all emotions and feelings, and, in return, memorize and regurgitate general rules and the exceptions therein, apply the facts to the law, and conclude. For me, the real learning experience came from the preparation classes, which precede the bar exam. Personally, I was not opposed to skipping law school all together, taking the bar preparation classes, and attempting the bar exam. Indeed, to pass the bar in this manner would be a great feat—if you were courageous and smart enough to attempt it.

As an older student, I had experienced enough of life to comprehend that taking an examination was the least of my worries. I had already buried my husband and suffered egregious sexual abuse at the hands of my father. What could possibly be so difficult about taking an exam? Cops pass the bar the first time around for the same reason. Police officers, especially those on patrol, experience the worst of what life has to offer while trying to stay alive. I mean this literally. What can possibly frighten a patrol cop at this point? No examination in the world could be as scary to them as the moments they roll out alone at night in some of the scariest parts of our city.

Jokingly, it is said, "There is nothing worse than taking the bar the first time than taking it the second." Although this is probably true, it still boils down to taking an examination. The brightest of the bright freeze up while others remain paralyzed by three years of unmitigated propaganda. I really blame most of the innate fear of law school on the hallowed professors. The instilled mentality is such that there are only a handful of students who can truly understand the law. Real teaching, however, would indeed be an improvement over the Socratic Method and an invaluable contribution to those who truly desire to study the law. Professors harass students through the Socratic Method of teaching. Too much time and energy is spent on asking inane questions while simultaneously, ruthlessly grilling the humbled students, now shriveled under their seats.

Some students already know that they have a job waiting for them after graduation, while the rest of us are clueless as to what we are going to do. Those with large student loans end up working for defense firms, papering opposing counsel into idiocy and the client into bankruptcy. There is no doubt that law school remains cutthroat; it appeals to those who are greedy and power hungry and often those without a moral compass. It is a certainty that law school perpetuates the likes of those already so inclined.

In summary, I never wanted to practice law. My own disdain for lawyers grew to an all-time high while in law school. A friend of mine talked me into taking the bar while the material was fresh in my head. If my goal were to be an effective and efficient businessperson, I was now swimming with the sharks. This was a huge mistake! A successful businessperson can, and usually does, function outside the constraints of the box. Having a law degree ensures that one can never leave the box without huge consequences: usually in the form of the dreaded state bar. Ergo, carried out each day are unethical, illegal, and immoral acts committed by attorneys while contained and constrained within the narrow parameters of the box. The courts themselves perpetuate this behavior because lawyers, supposedly officers of the court, consistently lie bold faced to judges and opposing counsel. Attorneys are not called upon to explain their blatant behavior or be held accountable for the violations of their own professional codes.

A WOMAN'S VIEWPOINT OF THE LAW

For All the Stage Is a Theater

The law is a jealous mistress—a statement that few doubt. Innately, women sense this more than men do. A woman understands that she must work two or three times as hard as a man must in an effort to break the stereotype of a "skirt." A man's attitude toward female opponents is conclusive and culturally determined. Women are believed to have a passive, secondary role in society. With women still looked upon as minor players, it is sexist. Men underestimate their female opponents. A man's biggest mistake is thinking a woman is brainless and patting her on the head with the usual, "Don't worry your pretty little head about it." Men, for the most part, under-prepare themselves for court appearances. Perhaps, stepping into battle, they are more comfortable winging an argument—which dates back to ancient times when a man's brawn most effectively guaranteed a win.

A woman who understands the inevitable battle between the sexes dresses for defense and aggression. Going to my closet, I give my choice of outfits all the care and deliberation a warrior might have given to his choice of armor. In my position, I consider dressing for defense every bit as important. Dressing as such is a show of force. Much like the warriors of olden times, I apply my makeup as carefully as war paint. In battles strictly against my opponent,

I find dark eyes and red lips work best along with my trademark Chanel suits, stilettos, Chanel Vamp polish and well-placed false eyelashes. In jury trials, we know from experience that soft colors, inexpensive clothes, worn shoes, and a Timex send a clear message that the attorney is trustworthy and will tell the client's story exactly as he or she wishes. The trial is not about the attorney but rather the client. It is always about the client. Even so, the courtroom is every bit the theater: costumes donned, lines memorized, and actors finely tuned for their delivery, perfectly aligned with stories to tell. The stage is set; a dramatic event unfolds.

A woman who is over-prepared will win easily. In the end, a flaming, defiant expression pierces the opponent's heart. This type of woman leaves the courtroom and steps into her limousine with a celebratory lemon drop martini. Not a spot of blood touches her Chanel suit.

There is no doubt that litigation is the last blood sport in civilization—closer to mortal combat than any other human intellectual activity. It is never a question of whether you have done the law right, but rather that as the victor, you are still standing in the pool of blood on the coliseum floor. Today, niceties and ethics fall by the wayside. The victor must succeed by any means possible, and the opponent must be eliminated. It is no longer sufficient that the victor captures the majority of the market share; he or she must ensure the opponent's termination. Litigation is indeed a very brutal sport: not for the faint of heart, soft-spoken or risk-averse. Litigation requires a well-rehearsed plan, quickness in sparring, and ultimately, a risk taker.

For the most part, attorneys are more successful if they are conservative. It is a cookie-cutter look that is accepted by other attorneys, judges, clients, and society. I have always been on the Gerry Spence side of the spectrum. The way I dressed exemplified my aggressive code of honor. My skill set is gritty, assiduous, and determined. I was an excellent student and attentive to detail. Now, I am a seasoned warrior; my skill set, well-honed. My colleagues remarked, "Mary Elizabeth was often imitated but never duplicated." I worked my profession much like a politician works a cocktail party. One of my law clerks was afraid that his association with me would taint him, based on my style. He understood that I was defiant to the standards of normalcy. It was funny that my style never bothered him in the beginning. Notably, it was my very style that attracted him to me in the first place. But like most male-female relationships, that which attracts in the beginning is the very thing that repulses them in the end.

MY PHILOSOPHY OF LAW

Every day, I gathered my strength to fight a battle that others, who have also sworn an oath to uphold, now no longer care about. Certainly, this is another factor that makes litigation such a dangerous sport.

I have an old-fashioned sense of responsibility—a personal sense of obligation to right wrongs. It is at the very heart of what motivates me and the single most potent influence in my life. My flaw is my spirit's unwillingness to let go—of not accepting the unwritten law of closure, which, despite the possibilities of appeals, is a necessary fact of the legal system: a safeguard against an endless round of rematches.

I possess an unwavering awareness of the vexed relationship between the objective truth and the narrative truth lawyers impose upon it. Herein lies the paradox: it is the perpetual and un-winnable battle between the objective truth and the narrative truth.

In trusting the truth to lawyers, the profession is always in violation of the objective truth—even if, in so doing, it contains no overt lies. The jury is dependent on lawyers. Yet, the raw truth (what the client has entrusted to his or her attorney) is often messy, emotional, incoherent, and oftentimes unsatisfying and boring—thus, the perceived need for betrayals and ultimately the inevitable loses inherent in the imposition of the narrative truth over the objective truth and the power struggles over who will impose it.

The betrayal of the client lies in the fact that a lawyer can never tell the client's story exactly as the client wants it told, but the lawyer promises implicitly or explicitly that he or she can.

My practice of the law was done with a purity of purpose: a single-mindedness that struck my colleagues as naïve, suspect, and at times, irksome. My personal philosophy, when actualized, was very simple because I fully understood the paradox. My belief, however, in the rightness of my own motives was a need so deeply rooted that, in the wrong circumstances, became a form of blindness.

At one point in my legal career, I made some simple resolutions. Litigation began to ware on me and on my health, and it began to show. My purpose and passion needed some reigning in before I suffered my first heart attack. One resolution was to practice a gentler, kinder law. Working in the underbelly of the courts, my mission was to eradicate vestiges of discrimination. Sometimes, it was difficult to avoid sparring with opposing counsel and the bad actors they represented.

It was not soon after my decision to practice a gentler law that I forced myself to put my resolutions on the shelf. The need to war against the ilk of those who make their living off the disillusioned, dispossessed, and disenfranchised enraged me. Mentally sighing, I climbed into my armor, unsheathed my battle sword, and held my shield over my heart, locking into battle, forgetting everything else—it was my father all over again. I knew this was going to get very personal.

It turned very personal for me in those cases where the women I represented were sexually harassed, raped, marginalized, demeaned, or degraded. Male employers rued the day they came within my laser vision. I was skilled at disassembling monsters. I ripped their hearts out for even thinking that these women were not a man's equal and targeting them as a plaything, without a serious thought in their heads, victimizing them until the pain was unbearable. There are thresholds of mental fatigue. I swore to avenge their honor. These men were no different from my father: bottom feeders for those they considered the weaker species. I knew everything I needed to know about each of these monsters; my aim was for the jugular. Prior to jousting, their headshots were backdrops for my dartboard. I never missed the mark.

Most of the people lawyers interact with are coarse human beings who fashion their careers from human dross. Lawyers have chosen a difficult profession. Initially, lawyers see a lot of peculiar behavior that they do not understand. As lawyers become more perceptive in their practice, they have witnessed most of man's peculiarities. It has led them to believe they can actually predict human behavior. As a profession, it is a form of delusion. Under any set of circumstances, lawyers pass harsh judgments against their fellow humans. The realities of life are very simple. A person can never really quite penetrate the truth of why some people do the strange things they do. The most we can do is look at one another with compassion: a reminder that none of us is exempt from error—sometimes-serious error. Thus, it is important to temper our judgments of others with humility and an understanding that we will always remain ignorant to certain matters within the heart.

It is a mistake to believe that a person is only one thing. The human personality is far too complex for such simplicity. It is indeed a rare individual who actually is as he or she appears to be. Most people are either more or less. At times, people willfully deceive us. Sometimes, we deceive ourselves. People are more comfortable with self-deception, not wanting to see reality because it is invariably complicated. Their daily masks are eventually melded to the wearers' personalities until they become the mask and that which now defines them. People prefer to keep things simple. It is a sin of pride that forces lawyers to believe they can fathom the absolutes of any person or situation. It is the practice of law which convinces lawyers into thinking that they can; it is an un-winnable proposition.

"THE SUBCONSCIOUS IS THE KEY TO ONE'S LIFE'S PURSUITS."
—Carl Jung

At seven years of age, I became fascinated with a well-known television show, *Perry Mason*, the longest-running lawyer show in American television history. The fascination was the notion of justice in an hour. In the middle of all the sexual abuse, I often wondered if there would be justice for me too. Was a grown-up going to save me? Would anyone even care enough about me to rescue me? For ten-plus years, I suspected God had abandoned me.

I wanted to be a judge when I grew up: a responsible grown-up who saw through the lies and injustices and helped those who could not help themselves. Television portrayed judges as honest, stern but kind, and knowledgable but compassionate. The portrayal of judges became an inspiration to me and represented what I wanted to become when I grew up.

As the years passed, I never lost sight of my dream. Granted, I did not have a political agenda or a source for major campaign contributions that would lead to a judicial appointment. My legal career consisted of teaching employment law and a practice of representing the disillusioned, dispossessed, and disenfranchised from discrimination and retaliation. I often appeared before the United States Equal Employment Opportunity Commission

(EEOC), representing complainants against federal employers who believed that they were above their own laws. A litigator at heart, I enjoyed the sheer challenge of righting wrongs. After appearing before the EEOC for almost ten years, I developed a respect for the mission of the Agency and they for me. I had the pleasure of appearing before some of the best judges in their field.

One day, I telephoned the Los Angeles District Office and inquired about the requirements and the necessary steps to become a federal administrative civil rights judge. I lived and breathed discrimination law and its practice. Discrimination law is the most difficult law to practice. The assumption is correct. The body of law encompassing discrimination is constantly in transition, being defined and refined by the agency and higher court rulings. I thanked the kind judge who took the time to speak with me and asked him to contact me if there were future openings. My telephone call to him, I suspect, was quite common and hardly memorable. Two years later, I received a return telephone call from the same judge. He was not asking me if I wanted the position, he was simply informing me that an announcement was open for application if I still wanted to become a judge. With the exception of childbirth and mothering, this was one of the biggest moments of my life. I realized the selection of a federal administrative judge was competitive; nonetheless, it was now within my reach. My dreams and desires remained earnest throughout the years.

Many factors go into the selection of a judge. Judges by definition must have a certain judicial temperament. A judge is unbiased: without favoritism for one side or the other. A judge establishes a level playing field for all parties. As a law professor and practitioner, I was uniquely qualified for possessing the proper judicial temperament. A judge must be very familiar with the federal rules of evidence and other rules of civil procedure. A judge must be able to write clear and concise decisions, manage a large caseload, and handle complex cases. This was, in fact, no different from my current practice of law.

When it came time for my interview, it is now embarrassing to admit that I was so nervous I forgot how to put my pantyhose on. It was a good thing my daughter was with me. Her sense of humor was greatly appreciated. Security in a federal building is ratcheted up compared to superior courts. Thus, my next embarrassing moment was setting off every alarm in the building. The United States Marshalls almost completely disrobed me until they discovered my shoes were the culprit. The better the quality the shoe, the more likely it was to set off an alarm. (well-made shoes are comprise of tacks or nails as opposed to glue.) Mortified by the very thought that my potential interviewers were behind me, I hurriedly dressed and quickly found the interview room. Lucky for me, not one of the interviewers were in line behind me. Truly, I was a nervous wreck. If you have ever wanted someone or something so badly in life, you understand the dynamics. It seemed as if every step was important—that is because it was!

The panel consisted of six judges. Each judge asked me questions from a predrafted list of questions. Following the final interview, the designated panel allowed me to ask any questions that I might have concerning the Agency. Over-preparing as usual for my interview allowed some comfort throughout the arduous and nerve-racking process. I had thoroughly researched all of the new and pending legislation involving the EEOC. The interview felt like it went well, but who knew.

My references were listed on the application form. Later, I discovered the following statements were made about me. Comments of this type always surprised me as I still struggled with my self-esteem. The dean of the law school said, "Mary Elizabeth was the brightest woman to ever walk through the doors of this law school";

colleagues relayed, "[She] was grace under fire"; "managed large caseloads"; and, by reputation, was "one of the top discrimination litigators in the United States." Regardless of how I ranked during the interview or how wonderful my references seemed, there was no reason for me to believe that either the interview or references placed me in the top five candidates.

I waited and waited to hear about the results. Anyone who understands the inner workings of the government will tell you that most everything advances at a snail's pace. When the supervising judge telephoned my office and asked to speak with me, I closed my office door while the rest of my office sat anxiously waiting for the results. My secretary, my legal assistant, and the only other attorney that worked for me placed their ears close to the door, hoping to hear something that gave an indication of whether I had been selected. When I opened the door of my office, my staff literally fell on top of me. They looked as scared as I felt when the telephone first rang. Apparently, they did not overhear anything. After unwinding our legs from each other's, they all started asking questions at once. I screamed so loud, you would have thought that I won the lottery. With great excitement and awe, I stated, "I got the job; I am going to be a judge!" We were all delirious with happiness. I made telephone calls; people gathered at the office; and I felt something I have never felt before: sheer, unmitigated happiness. It was the most intoxicating moment of my life. We closed the office and celebrated!

The first question my staff asked was what took me so long to express any emotion behind closed doors. I explained that I asked about the salary—something that I had not been concerned with before the application process. I was shocked at how little the federal government paid. When the interviewing judge

"The Subconscious Is The Key To One's Life's Pursuits."

heard the hesitation in my voice, he quickly stated that he would submit a request for a higher salary based on my outstanding achievements, education, and litigation experience, and that I would receive promotions every year. I still had some concerns when he relayed that it was way below the amount I usually earned—scarily so. Whacking a zero from my hourly rate would be a challenge for even the best of budgeters. As a woman, I had developed a love affair for Manolo Blahnik shoes. There would be no money for extras at all, including a former madness for shoes. No one—and I mean no woman—who works for the federal government can afford shoes that begin at five hundred dollars. None of this mattered to me now. In the split second he told me about the salary, I decided my discretionary spending was irrelevant.

What mattered was that I sought and found my dream: a way to have a greater impact in our nation, protecting those who were less capable of protecting themselves. I was now in a position to make case law through my own legal decisions which, if challenged, would become legal precedent.

My appointment was the single most fulfilling career accomplishment in my life. It rocked my world. I could not believe it for some time into the future. I do not know how others handle news of this proportion, but I was both honored and humbled. This feeling never dissipated. My lifelong dream was a reality. My spirituality led to a plan; I used every visionary tool in my arsenal to work the plan, and the plan came to fruition. Never doubt that the most unlikely dream can become your very reality.

BIRTH OF THE EEOC

The EEOC was legislatively mandated as the "model employer," designated to eradicate all vestiges of discrimination. The mission of the agency, according to my initial indoctrination, was to ensure that federal employees were able to work in an environment free of discrimination and retaliation.

The EEOC was created in the mist of the historic Civil Rights Act of 1964. While I fought off my father, the fight for civil rights equality played out in the streets of America. In 1963, President John F. Kennedy addressed the nation on television. I will never forget Kennedy's speech. He was eloquent in his words, and his message, although simple, was profound:

> We are confronted primarily with a moral issue. It is as old as the scriptures, and it is clear as the American Constitution. The heart of the question is whether all Americans are afforded equal rights and equal opportunities, whether we are going to treat our fellow Americans as we want to be treated.... [O]ne hundred years of delay have passed since President Lincoln freed the slaves, yet their heirs, their grandsons, are not fully free. They are not yet free from

the bonds of injustice. In addition, this nation for all its hopes and all its boasts will not be fully free until all of its citizens are free....

The growing racial unrest in the country was flashed across televisions everywhere. I was horrified by the violence that erupted from the demonstrations. The protests evidenced and exposed egregious and pervasive racial discrimination and

segregation. Television clearly demonstrated the country's profound unrest throughout the nation. The protests and demonstrations captured the atmosphere of urgency. Americans became enraged at what they saw and heard. In the spring of 1963, television exposed that peaceful demonstrators were beaten—including children—attacked by police dogs, sprayed with high-pressure water hoses, arrested, and jailed. Our image abroad was tainted by the civil unrest.

It was during this period of history we see the most amazing heroic leaders: John F. Kennedy, Martin Luther King, and his son, Martin Luther King Jr. According to the EEOC itself, these remarkable men as named above and women such as Rosa Parks left a mark on how we experience racial issues. The images of the protesters and beatings galvanized the nation by confronting it with its own failures.

I was thirteen years of age when I first witnessed this incredible battle. I embraced the struggle for civil rights as if it were my own. I was shocked by the reality that not all Americans were treated equally in their employment, in housing, in voting, and in education because of their color and race.

On August 28, 1963, approximately 250,000 Americans of all races descended on Washington, DC. It was then that Dr. Martin

Luther King came forward and indelibly marked the souls of Americans in his "I Have a Dream" speech. His words were powerful, and Americans were hungry for meaningful actions to back Kennedy's insistence for legislation. The demand for racial equality and justice coalesced with the civil rights movement. A strong presidential leadership led to the passage of the Civil Rights Act of 1964.

I will always remember the image of Martin Luther King as he stood on the steps of the Lincoln Memorial and demanded the rights to vote, fair housing, equal pay and the right to attend integrated schools. Embedded in my memory is the picture of King's hands outstretched, wearing a dark tie and French cuffs, as he waved to a sea of people so thick it seemed to go on forever. Martin Luther King Jr., every inch his father's son and spokesperson, profoundly stated that people are to be judged not "by the color of their skin but by the content of their character."

I wept for those who peacefully attempted to wake up all Americans to this reality. In Kennedy's speech of 1963, he said:

> Now the time has come for this nation to fulfill its promise. The events of Birmingham and elsewhere have so increased the cries for equality that no city or state or legislative body can prudently ignore them. We face, therefore, a moral crisis as a country and as a people. It cannot be met with repressive police action. It cannot be left to increased demonstrations on the streets. It cannot be quieted by token moves or talk. It is time to act in Congress, in your state and local legislative body, and above all, in all of our daily lives....

Kennedy asked Congress to make a commitment to the proposition that race has no place in American life or law.

Congressional opposition for the passage of civil rights laws was fierce. The bias and prejudices of our Congress did not go by unnoticed, evidenced by Congress's debate over whether all Americans should have an equal opportunity regardless of their race or color.

The passage of the Civil Rights Act of 1964 came about with bullhorns and the footsteps of thousands of feet on pavement. The EEOC was designated as the federal agency to enforce these rights. The EEOC began operations officially on July 2, 1965, but it was a powerless organization. Progress towards equality for all was slow. Congress held public hearings on proposed amendments to Title VII, the Civil Rights Act. In their meetings, they discovered that there was widespread and rampant discrimination in the private and public sectors. Blacks, women, and minorities made precious little progress. As a result, Congress empowered the EEOC to legislate, enforce, and hold judicial hearings. These were the times that signaled that race based issues were ripe, someone or something had to change. To date, we have definitely made progress but the race based issues have become elastic with immigration and mixed race marriages. Today's dialogue is not driven solely by black Americans but a plethora of races where discrimination is alive and well in all endeavors, especially the employment arena.

Throughout my tenure as a civil rights judge I heard heart wrenching and heartfelt stories, painful and raw. Oftentimes what I heard was appalling and shocking. Complainants were candid about the egregious discrimination by the federal government. I heard the pain, anger, guilt, regret, defeat, the disappointments, resentments and the fears of retaliation (inevitable from employers accused of violating human and civil rights). Justice is now illusory as employers use cheap litigation tactics to manipulate even the strongest truths, unquestionable factual evidence and the interpretation of the law. Invariably, employers intentionally destroy decent, hard-working people who had the courage and the right to speak up and came forward. Why? It is all about the money. Complainants and plaintiffs are awarded damages when the employer has been found liable for discrimination and retaliation.

America is ever changing, and now requires a different kind of courage – to eradicate the corruption found in every level of government, employment and in our court systems. We must ask and answer the following question: where are the real heroes today? The American economy has been decimated. Almost 50 years later it is unfortunate that the power given to government officials and those, in particular, who were to enforce our civil rights has turned power into shameless abuses, illegal government practices, and corruption. What I experienced and heard as a judge changed my life forever. It is tragic that Kennedy is not here today. I believe he too would say that corruption has no place in American life or law. This is another story – best left to another day.

FULL CIRCLE
The Power of Choices

When first asked to write this book, I was told that it might trigger painful memories. My response was very simple: "When you have been violently abused for ten-plus years, those memories are always present"—sometimes front and center. There are some things that we simply do not get past without walking through them—eyes wide open. Certainly, any attempt at blocking them, stuffing them, or believing an end-run around them will work is simply a delusion. One way or another, you must take this walk; granted, you must take it alone, and it can be very disturbing, chaotic, and just plain depressing. Until you have been through the crucible of life, your mettle cannot be tested. My way is certainly not the only way, but it does make sense of what, for most of us, is utterly senseless. Kahlil Gibran said, "Say not that I have found the truth, but rather I have found *a* truth." It is in the spirit of this quotation that I have proffered my heart and soul to you in speaking my truth.

Those struggling through issues of abuse are undertaking a massive conscious transformation. We collectively understand that our old ways of thinking and acting are no longer effective. We entered the evolutionary transformation process because we found ourselves to be limited in our thinking. Now, through this process, we have entered a more expansive understanding of who we are and of the yet-to-be-discovered unlimited, unmet potential.

A fierce resistance rises up from the old ways we chose to manage our lives. The old ways are still deeply embedded in our consciousness. This resistance emerges just as the metamorphic changes evolve. A raging battle ensues as we engage in the change to a higher consciousness. There is a fierce conflict between these two forces. Those who are violated struggle even harder as the old ways of coping brought with them defense mechanisms. These mechanisms are outdated and serve no one, but they did work at some point, and we are reluctant to let them go.

There is an attempt to resist the call to a higher level of consciousness which has not yet been enlightened by the evolutionary process and is still stagnating. The old eventually gives way to the new; the new becomes old; and so it goes. This metamorphic transformation is how we evolve.

Chaos and conflict precede the new. While the process works its way to fruition, we experience ongoing contractions as the metamorphic process transforms itself into its new evolutionary expansion.

We are writing our own stories as we make choices. Those choices that are life-enhancing help us to elevate the soul to a higher consciousness, while those choices which are life-diminishing keep us from evolving into who we were meant to be. Regardless of our choices, it creates a ripple effect in ourselves and to others in the world around us.

In the tapestry of life, every thread woven into the whole is unique. You may feel that your contribution is small and insignificant in the scheme of things, but we could not produce the new without your thread. If everyone thought his or her contribution of no use, we could never complete what was meant to be. You may extend this point of view cosmically as humankind evolves. We are microcosms in the bigger picture. This is one reason why our personal choices have a universal ripple effect, as there are even greater consequences to what we do and become.

As you probably guessed, my story does not have a fairy tale ending: there is no glass slipper for this Cinderella. Life is simply not fair; to believe that it could be was delusional on my part. For some of us, there are realities that never level out, give us a break, or lend us a hand before the next invasive assault. I know what this looks and feels like. As a child, I remember blow-up dolls that were weighted at the bottom. Once these dolls were hit, they sprung right back up again.

Pretend you had this doll all your life, and every time you took a sock in the nose, the doll took a blow. After some thirty or forty years of this bludgeoning, the doll rose up—but ever so slowly. The doll lost its resiliency; once hardy, it too has taken too many punches. The point remains that the doll still rises to the challenge—even if a little slower. We are like the doll. We keep coming back, no matter how dark and depraved the circumstances. Some people are born with a hardiness of constitution and a resiliency to life that others do not have. A sexually abused child's ability to be resilient or hardy is weakened from abuse. True, it starts out with an enormous handicap, but nonetheless, the soul can be strong. I cannot explain why some people's souls remain un-singed or end up with a scratch instead of scar.

This knowledge grants us power—more power than you can imagine. It is an indicator of what we still need to do. This process will help self-indicate who and how you will interact with those around you and what and how you take care of your basic needs, including your sanity—all in an effort to provide a protective bubble around you so that healing can begin. We all need this bubble. No matter where I am or how bad my reality is, I think of myself in my pink bubble.

My office manager drew a picture of me inside a pink bubble. It was here that I stood, untroubled by the chaotic world around me. She saw me work until I could no longer stand and watched me suffer one blow after another. She decided that this warrior needed a break on occasion, so she surprised me by drawing this kindergarten-like picture to place above my computer. After relocating a half-dozen times, I no longer have the picture, but I always return to the vision of this pink bubble for nurturing and nourishing—even today. It has kept my sanity intact more times than you know.

You, my dear reader, have become my friend. I envision that you are a marvelous, unrepeatable, and sparkling jewel. You, too, had the courage to forge ahead, and you took this journey with me; most likely, you could script my ending.

You never expected me to jump up and tell you that after so many "Mr. Wrongs," I finally found "Mr. Right." My pursuit for justice and fair play is fierce; helping others is the commitment I have made to better my life and those lives around me.

In reality, I am content with my life. I live alone with my white standard poodle, "Ms. Too Divine." In her eyes, I am without fault; she loves me unconditionally. That means a lot to me. Oddly enough, I am fine living alone. I could never settle for someone not remotely close to what I need as a woman or make do. Life is way too short for that nonsense. I miss the creature comforts of having a partner in my life—someone to share the day's events, celebrate victories, or to tell me everything is going to work out when I cannot see the forest through the trees. I do not want a man I could run over, nor do I want a man who wants to fix me—I am not broken. He cannot solve my problems by taking out the CEO, buying his company, or working him over *mano a mano*. If anyone needs to deal with the challenges in my life, that person will be me. I need someone who is rock solid, who possesses the common sense that I do not always bring to the table, who loves me because of who I am and where I have been, and who appreciates who I am today. It is a little too late for anyone to think I could be changed by someone else's actions; I must change myself. I am a compelling person in my own right. The question is: how did this woman go through so much and still stand strong fearlessly fighting for the rights of others—let alone be so articulate, compassionate, passionate, and loving? It beats the hell out of me.

There is no doubt that my reader understands—because he or she is I. Thankfully, in taking this journey beside me—as horrific, atrocious, dark, and depraved as the ride was—we made it through the darkness. I can still be afraid when life blindsides me, but my fears are tamed. Acting out? Not so much. Beating myself up for life's vagaries? Still some. Nothing, and I mean nothing, is what it used to be. Today, my life makes sense; I have something valuable to offer; and I am loved and appreciated for who I am.

In the end, the outcome of this journey had some wonderful benefits. Now, my dear reader, I am quietly going to leave you to live your life. I am praying that, in the touching of my soul, it makes your journey easier. No soul is the same; make your life uniquely your own. Now, I will go back and live my life and work on myself some more until I get it right.

Thanks to every one of my readers, the healing process has made giant strides, and I am a better person for having journeyed through it with you. I will miss you. You—the collective you—inspired me. I cannot thank you enough. One day, we will meet again: when you tell me your story, how you managed your challenges, and who you have become. My next book will be about you—your unlimited potential and how you survived the challenges. This will be a very exciting book for me to write; I look forward to it, my friends. You gifted me with courage. I pray I gifted you with hope—hope for change, for redemption, and for new beginnings and second chances.

For those who wish to share their stories, please write to honorablejudgebullock@gmail.com.

Made in the USA
Lexington, KY
20 September 2017